I

AM

GLORY

BREAKING THROUGH OBSCURITY

U.K. Tommy

ISBN: 978-978-989-858-9

DEDICATION

This book is dedicated to anyone intending to break free from poverty and disappointment. The idea behind this book is to provide a guide for whoever desires a life of glory after accepting Jesus Christ as Lord and Saviour.

It is also dedicated to all who have tutored me tirelessly in the things of God over the years, those who have modeled true Christian Character and have shared their experiences and testimonies with me.

My dear wife has been a very patient and supportive friend particularly when I was putting together this lucubration of information, experiences, thoughts and messages from the Holy Spirit.

May all who seek, find and be transformed through the proven principles offered by this book, in order to live in total victory and in accordance with God's plan for His children.

CONTENTS

FOREWORD

Ubong Kingsley Tommy is singularly qualified to write this book "I Am Glory: Breaking through obscurity". His very name "Ubong" means Glory. Since He joined our local church at the Mount Zion Lighthouse Full Gospel Church, Karshi, Abuja FCT, he has been consistent in his diligent seeking of the truth and has been committed to the service of faith and the gospel of Jesus Christ for which he was ordained a Pastor.

His book is a gentle guide into a personal experience in a holy relationship and walk with a holy God which has brought and will always bring great success, breakthrough and victory leading to a life of peace and hope. He has used a simple and contemporary writing style that is smooth and rather poetic. In chapter six, he carefully brought out the wisdom benefits of spreading the Good News while chapter seven aptly cautions against the carelessness of taking profanity for freedom, which seems to be the order of the day.

This book which does not leave its reader in any illusion as to God's love for His special children — those who love and obey His word, places them in a special group of those who carry God's presence with them and as such their lives are victorious, successful in all things and inaccessible by the devices of the evil one.

As a Bible scholar, I would like to congratulate Ubong for this informative and insightful book. It is surely a contribution to the knowledge and fear of God.

Bishop E.U Ekwere (Rear Admiral Rtd)
Superintendent Abuja Diocese/Zonal Bishop
Mount Zion Lighthouse Full Gospel Church, Jahi, FCT Abuja,
Nigeria.
(2020)

CHAPTER 1
First Things First

"But seek ye first the kingdom of God..."
-        *Jesus Christ*

It was 2008, and finally, my opportunity had come. After almost a decade of teaching and desiring a change, I finally secured a new job in the capital, Abuja.

Abuja, Nigeria's capital, with its wide roads laced with several pedestrian and motor bridges, was at the time growing at a fast pace, and many government and non-government agencies were setting up offices across the city, which meant an opportunity for green grass seekers.

I was one of those who had grabbed well-paid employment in one of the reputable organisations and was excited to take up residence and start a new career journey that would shape the rest of my life. Like many, life in the capital had captivated me. Observing the crowds and seemingly endless queues of cars seen during rush hour, I saw opportunities everywhere.

For instance, even traffic jams were an opportunity for many people to trade in wares and make a buck here and there. The high cost and sophistication of almost everything were enough to captivate any young mind, and I still wondered what the future held for me.

I soon rented a small comfortable house in one of the estates, where I enjoyed support and favour from my landlord and his wife. My new life had begun; my uncertain future was unfolding. From then on, it was from one blessing to another. The next four years were spent enjoying the life I had eventually gotten accustomed to. Then suddenly, things began to change where I worked, which left me jobless. So, by the end of the fifth year, I had fallen into hard times that came with a steady retrogression, loaded with blows of want and lack.

In my growing despair, I found no relief from either friend or drink. Suddenly, the days seemed longer, and I spent more time thinking. My dear father of blessed memory had had many such experiences in his lifetime, and I interrogated my mind, trying to remember our conversations on how he got through them.

He was a praying man. I wondered what made the prayers he offered different to mine as I had on several occasions knelt to ask for divine intervention in my troubles, but nothing happened.

One day, after I had moved out of my nice neighbourhood and into a remote part of town, I received a call from a former colleague who pleaded that I help drive her mother, who had newly moved into a house within my vicinity, to church for a fellowship. That was something my good nature allowed me to do, but there was one problem- one problem that I did not know how to mention to this colleague, and it was that my petrol tank was almost empty.

"Well, it's just a one-time thing", I thought to myself as I pulled out of the corner of my uncompleted bungalow and into the dusty road of the secluded estate where I lived. I was on my way to my colleague's mother's house.

My favourite television show at the time was one in which the judge used to say, "No good deed goes unpunished", and as I drove, I hoped I wouldn't regret my decision.

We had just pulled into the church compound when I heard her mother ask if I would like to come into the church for a while, and with thoughts racing through my defiant mind, I declined. After all, the plan was to drop her off and not attend the fellowship with her. I was just not ready for all that, and as I drove off, a voice deep down kept telling me, "You should have accepted her invitation" It was so clear I needed God. A couple of fellowships later, having warmed up my feet, I finally decided to attend - a decision that would kick-start the change coming into my life. On that day, I was seated somewhere behind as the meeting progressed. I did not do much from where I sat but watched until it was time to pray. The prayer session was heated, and I said in my heart, "what I need right now is a job so that I can get out of difficulty and a wife so that I can put my sins behind me".

I wanted to serve God, but I needed to overcome the myriad challenges and addictions in my life first; I desperately needed help. Also, during this fellowship, I believe the Holy Spirit heard my every prayer, as my heart laid bare before Him, so He sent words to me. He located me in the crowd and said: "you came here to ask for a job and a wife, but I am offering something else in which you will find all these things" And that was it!- My opportunity to get back on track in my walk with God.

The decision I made that day turned out to be my most impactful. It was a day that I will never forget, one in which I learned how powerful the scripture that says: "Come, let us return to the LORD. He has torn us to pieces; now He will heal us, He has injured us; now He will bandage our wounds" (Hosea 6:1).

You see, many people spend their lives seeking everything but God. In their quest, they sustain lots of bumps and bruises. For a second, imagine a horse and a cart. You will agree that a carriage is supposed to be fitted behind the horse and drawn wherever it goes. The Bible says: "But seek first the kingdom of God, and His righteousness and all these things shall be added unto you" (Mathew 6:33). Now let's draw a quick analogy by considering the kingdom of God and His righteousness to be the horse and all other things, the cart. It certainly follows that with the cart fitted behind the horse, we can be sure that as long as the horse moves and wherever it goes, the cart follows. In trying to live a life of glory, we must understand that while we run after God and concern ourselves with taking care of kingdom business, the good things of life run after us, and God takes care of our business.

This concept is so profound that it can change anybody's life. It is also so practicable that it can be taught and must be first on the list of lessons to teach to those who truly wish to walk with God.

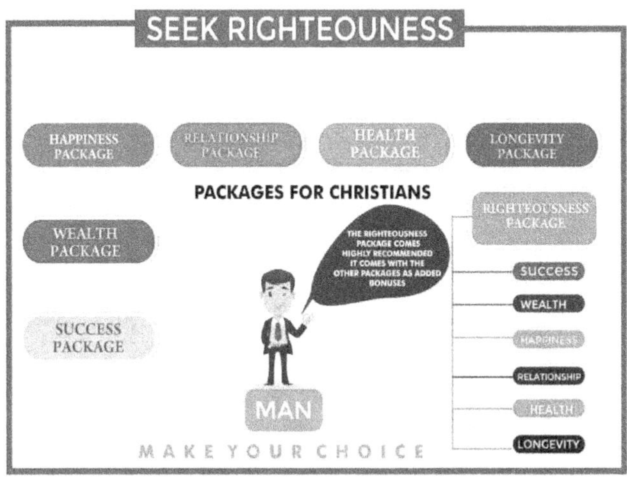

The Righteousness Package

When we seek the kingdom of God, what we get is called: "The Blessing", which is like a magnet that attracts all we need. Abraham received it, and it transformed his life. It made him wealthy and delivered the deepest desire of his heart to him - Isaac. The blessing is still powerful and available to us today and can be gotten when we do the things necessary to get God's attention. He is eager to manifest Himself on behalf of men with obedient hearts (2 Chronicles 16:9).

The kingdom of God is righteousness, peace and joy in the Holy Ghost. It is not a location but a state where we are likely to experience God. It is when we truly begin to live victoriously through our faith in the Lord. It is a realm of glory where we can take our places as children of God. Let's look at what it takes to operate in that realm.

SEEK RIGHTEOUSNESS

To seek righteousness means to strive to be more like God in character. Among the traits of God's character are faithfulness, holiness, impartiality, mercy and slowness to anger.

The word righteousness appears two hundred and six times in the Old Testament. It also appears seventy-nine times in the New Testament. Righteousness refers to our behaviour and how we live our lives. The journey to righteousness starts with surrendering our lives to God. Also, when we become true Christians, we become judicially declared righteous.

So whenever we hear the words "The righteous", It's us! The righteous live by faith. Through this faith, they tap into the work of redemption by Jesus on the cross. Leadership should therefore be the resolve of the righteous – those with God's kind of character because when this quality, the people rejoice. So, in whatever sphere, leaders should be chosen carefully from men with tested Godly character (Proverbs 29:2).

If anyone has fallen away from righteousness, there is restoration in the waiting, on the altar of prayer. Only God can restore us to righteousness if we fervently pray and seek His face (Job 33:26).

SEEK PEACE

Father Abraham's grandson- Jacob, was a man of peace. A successfully dug water well back in his day was an important property. Its usefulness to the sustenance of life made it an asset worth fighting for, but Jacob was too peaceful to do so. At one time, he had to forfeit two wells to ensure peace, and at another frowned at the actions of two of his sons, who angrily killed all the men in a host-town.

One Christian sister explained to me how much of a warrior she was and how it was necessary to deal with devils spiritually and physically when I tried to speak to her about how troublesome she had become. Violence, thuggery and destruction should not be left behind by any Christian. That is not what we are called to do. God is never pleased when we destroy what He loves. Can you remember that Bible passage, widely used and quoted during evangelism that tells how much God loved the world? (John 3:16).

God expects us to turn from all our evil and not just enjoy the existing peace around us but pursue it through deliberate actions. What we must do in these actions is not just expect peace but be part of working out the peace we would like to see. That may require a lot of sacrifice in addition to knowing and trusting God. It's the assurance of His power to provide for us and judge on our behalf. Knowing this should help us let go of offences and embrace peace (Psalm 34:14).

SEEK A RELATIONSHIP WITH THE HOLY SPIRIT

The Holy Spirit, also known as the Holy Ghost, is God's spirit and the third member of His trinity nature (Father, Son and Spirit). Though we cannot see him, His personality is sensed and enjoyed by all true believers.

The Holy Spirit is a gift from God to believers. Jesus earned Him for us through His work of redemption on the cross (Ephesians 2:8).

Knowing the Holy Spirit fills our lives with power, and when He fills our lives, we begin to experience victories we did not achieve (Zachariah 4:6).

The Holy Spirit was present during the seven days of creation. He enlightened and inspired the prophets of the Old Testament and gave power to priests and kings to function. Remember also that Jesus was conceived by the Holy Spirit, who also descended upon Him and anointed Him for His earthly ministry.

One Bible Scholar argued that the book of Acts in the Bible should have been named the "Acts of the Holy Spirit". The Holy Spirit moved very mightily in the lives of the twelve apostles, which led to the establishment of the church.

As mentioned earlier, the Holy Spirit has a personality because He shows emotion in reaction to our actions and inactions. If we get Him to befriend us, we derive ten powerful benefits that guarantee the earlier spoken victories in our lives.

Benefit 1: Divine assistance

The Holy Spirit is a comforter, advocate, counsellor and helper. He usually speaks in that still and small voice that tells you not to take that wrong or wicked decision.

We can be sure of living above depression when we have the Holy Spirit because He feeds our spirit with the joy of the Lord that strengthens us in all circumstances (John 14:16).

Benefit 2: Unlimited knowledge

Everything that Jesus taught or wants to tell us, is released by the Holy Spirit. He also teaches those connected to Him all they need to know (John 14:26).

He provides all the knowledge we need to fulfil our purpose. He also helps us make an impact. That should not be surprising because He knows all things. Don't let anyone tell you differently because the Holy Spirit was with God the Father from the beginning.

Benefit 3: Testimony of Jesus

The Holy Spirit, described above as an advocate, is also a testifier of the work of Jesus Christ. The Spirit of Truth, as the Bible also calls Him, speaks about Jesus to us (John 15:26).

I have heard Him speak about events at creation, the early prophets, the crucifixion and death of Christ Jesus and His resurrection.

Benefit 4: Enables conversion

The Holy Spirit can lead us to Christ Jesus. After preaching the message of repentance, only He can enable the work of conversion (Romans 8:14).

That is so because nobody can come to Jesus except God the Father draws him. That is made possible by the Holy Spirit (John 6:44).

Benefit 5: Impartation of God's nature

To be like God, we must first know Him. The Holy Spirit provides all the knowledge we require and helps us, through faith, to become more like Him.
If we allow God to fill us with His power, He, through His Spirit, can transform our very existence.

Benefit 6: Guidance

The sixth benefit of the Holy Spirit is guidance, which He provides to True Christians. He speaks the mind of God the Father and even tells of things to come.

Many of the goings-on today get revealed to the church beforehand to enable them proactively deal with challenges and appreciate the all-knowing nature of God. The Holy Spirit guides us and helps us walk in the will of God the Father.

Benefit 7: Witnessing our sonship

The Holy Spirit agrees with our spirit that we are children of God. He does this through the word of God. He also provides us with knowledge, advocacy, comfort, counsel and help (Romans 8:16).

As people called out of their previous lives and into one of service and obedience, the spirit of God speaks to us about this calling and our overall duty of love too. He also helps us get back on track in our walk with God.

Benefit 8: Intercession

The Bible says we do not know how to pray, but the Holy Spirit always helps us. Many people have testified how He wakes them up to pray at times critical for their victory.

He also helps us when we speak in tongues. He does this because we lack the knowledge of how or what to pray. He intervenes when we gather to pray and causes miraculous occurrences.

Benefit 9: Release of power

The power to do the miraculous comes from the Holy Spirit. He gives gifts to the church that guarantees the release of His power to do impossible things. This power leads to the restoration of sight to the blind, the opening of deaf ears, the healing of the sick, the raising of the dead and the ability to give powerful sermons that lead to repentance (Acts 1:8).

He also gives the power to live above all forms of affliction and curses because He can quicken the bodies of believers where He resides (Romans 8:11).

The power released by the Holy Spirit can be transferred to not just people but materials like handkerchiefs, which we can send anywhere to heal the sick and deliver the oppressed, as practised by the early Christians.

Churches like mine (The Mount Zion Lighthouse Full Gospel Church) allow the use of oil and water. It also allows a move of the Holy Spirit, like at Pentecost times (Acts 19:11-12).

Benefit 10: Deposits God's spirit in us

When we become born again, we receive a deposit of the Holy Spirit, who begins to dwell in us and enables us to do all the good we do.

Jesus told His disciples to wait in Jerusalem until the Comforter is received by them. That was because He knew how much power would be released. Jesus also knew how in His absence, the Comforter (Holy Spirit) could be received by several of His disciples at one time. That would facilitate the miracles in the tasks ahead of them.

Having the Spirit of God in us guarantees God's anointing. Like Jesus, whom the Bible describes as one who went about doing good, we become empowered to carry out the activities He spoke about while launching the great commission (Matthew 28:18-20).

Jesus confirms His words. He does this through signs and wonders, performed by the power released through the Holy Spirit (Mark 16:16-20 NIV).

CHAPTER 2
Building Reverential Fear

*"Children, Fear God; that is to say, have an holy awe
upon your minds to avoid that which is evil, and a strict
care to embrace and do that which is good"*

- *William Penn*

I had pondered many times about the lifestyle of living in fear of the Lord. I wondered what it was about. It was not uncommon to be quizzed by church leaders to ascertain how God-fearing you were. I remember feeling disobliged by questions aimed at discovering how God-fearing I was. One of those times was when I wanted to get married.

You will observe that marriage seminars usually end with participants deciding that the most required quality sought in people intending to get married is that of being God-fearing. Many have mistaken this quality to mean being an active member of a local church or being regular at gatherings. Others even attribute being God-fearing to those who hold church offices but believe me, I have seen many who fit into all the mentioned categories fall short of the true definition of being God-fearing.

The importance of wisdom to a person who wishes to live a life of glory cannot be overemphasized. Small wonder the Bible contains copious wisdom nuggets aimed to guide thought, decision making and action.

The process of becoming wise starts with a reverential fear of the Lord, but how can you fear Him if you do not believe He exists? Do you see His wondrous creations? Have you experienced His power? You surely must have heard someone speak about His greatness. How about the many mysteries that have remained unexplainable by scientists? Certainly, we must all have come from somewhere and will eventually return; don't you think? Atheism wasn't popular where I came from, as only a fool would deny God after growing up with the kind of experiences we had (Psalm 14:1).

I once knew someone who became amazed after witnessing a miracle of healing. For lack of appropriate words, this person kept muttering the word "Unbelievable!" And I responded by saying, "Believe it" That was just the first step that would be followed by getting to know the doer of the unbelievable personally. It can only happen if the choice to pursue wisdom is made instead of a continued life of foolishness in which we choose to ignore the Lord.

To Know the Lord personally starts from

believing that He exists and that there are rewards for fearing Him, which can add a lot of value to our lives of glory (Hebrews 11:6).

After which, it makes a lot of sense to examine how God rewards. So here we go. Let us review the lives of those who had experienced these rewards. Two women in the Bible acted bravely, driven by their fear of God and the desire to do what was right.

The fear of the Lord, explained in simple terms, means to hate and avoid whatever is evil (Proverbs 8:13). Certainly, a person who fears the Lord avoids a lifestyle that puts up a proud appearance. Such a person would know that, among other things, God hates pride (Proverbs 6:10-19). Moreso, because there is a strong relationship between pride and arrogance, people ought to embrace humility to avoid being irritants to God.

The Lord also hates the shedding of innocent blood, an occurrence so often these days. God gets upset when we destroy the work of His hands-man. So, with all the abortions, mass murders, armed robberies and terrorism of our day, every innocent life taken offends the creator.

In a local crime television programme I used to like so much, one of the characters explained why he joined a group of robbers. He spoke about how he came into financial difficulty and urgently needed money with nobody to help him. I bet that a million people must have been in a similar position at least once in their lives but resisted the temptation of turning to crime. It is all about the choices we make, I discovered.

One of my primary school teachers was fond of saying to us: "Rome wasn't built in a day" Which to me, pointed to the importance of being patient concerning the things of life. In addition to being patient, we should always pray and seek counsel before taking steps.

The Lord always makes a way where none seems to exist. The truth is that in such situations, you will notice that something always comes up. Life has taught many people how temporary and often worthless taking the seemingly easy way out by turning to sex, crime or drugs is.

Also, seeking peace at all times and avoiding emotions like jealousy, gossip and falsehood ensure that our actions do not lead to divisions and strife in our communities. That is because all of these require lies and evil devices, first concocted in our hearts, and then manifested in our speech and actions. They are capable of destroying us.

The fear of the Lord makes us avoid all these things. It assembles an alarm system in our hearts that goes off whenever we veer off God's course. We must develop this consciousness to full maturity if we want to live a God-fearing life.

THE REWARD FOR BEING GOD-FEARING

Living a God-fearing life pleases our Lord. It is more than a decision. It is a duty all of God's creation to perform (Ecclesiastes 12:13). This fear, which I always make a case for, is not like the one we have for the things that cause bodily harm, but it is a reverential way of living, to receive God's approval. As I had stated earlier, it comes with rewards, and there are experiences and stories to support this.

Let us consider the story of the two midwives. (Exodus 1:17-21). The Bible records that a powerful Egyptian king tried to control the population growth of the Hebrew people in his kingdom by asking two midwives, who helped Hebrew women give birth to their babies, to kill all male babies. Can you imagine how much damage losing sons would have done to families back then? That was wrong and meant shedding innocent blood, which the midwives were unwilling to get involved. So, they tactfully let the babies live.

These women took risks. They could have received severe punishments for refusing to do the evil instruction of the king. They, by their actions, qualify as models of people who have shown what it means to live God-fearing lives. The Lord rewarded them for what they did. He was good to them and blessed them with families of their own.

I had come to know Favour (not her real name) while visiting my parents-in-law. She was a single lady who can best be described as tall, dark and energetic. We never really spoke much, but I remember always thanking her for doing one thing or the other for me or showing me where to find stuff. She would often come around after church on Sundays or whenever there was an occasion to help the old folks out. To the best of my recollection, her demeanour was always that of a happy and dedicated helper.

After some years, my parents-in-law passed on and there she was again, mourning like family and doing all she could to help out. We had gathered ourselves to pray in preparation for the funeral when the Lord spoke to us. He promised to reward her for all her help and give her a family. These were rewards for all the love she had shown to the old folks, which had pleased Him.

We certainly can learn a lot from these stories. We cannot destroy others and what they hold dear and expect preservation. I have seen women who desired children but acted very wickedly towards the children of others. I knew one such woman who was so wicked to her maid that neighbours started talking. She ended up never having a child of her own. One practice in many Nigerian cultures is to refer to a mother with the prefix "Mama" followed by the name of either her first, last or popular child. So, let's say, for instance, the name of the first child of a woman is Mandy, she would likely be known as: "Mama Mandy", And that was how the woman in the story was called, with the name of the child to whom she acted wickedly, since she had none of her own.

I have also met a woman trusting the Lord for a child and served the Children's Department in Church with joy and all her heart. Despite being quite advanced, she became pregnant and birthed a healthy child. God's reward is for only those who fear Him, and this simple understanding can powerfully change even the most hopeless situation.

THE SPIRIT OF THE FEAR OF THE LORD

To create a better understanding, let us consider the words: "Spirit of" And replace them with: "Power to". So when we say the spirit of the fear of God, it can also mean the power to fear God. That is because when the Spirit of God comes upon us, we receive the power to perform.

The Bible, the second verse of the eleventh chapter of Isaiah, tells of four pertinent spirits given to a king chosen by God, and on this list, we will find out that it includes the spirit of the fear of the Lord.

The Lord thought it was important for the king to have the spirit of wisdom and understanding, the spirit of counsel and might, and the spirit of knowledge and He also felt it very necessary for the king to have the spirit of the fear of the Lord. The reason for that decision is what we will discuss next as the eight benefits of the spirit of the fear of the Lord.

Benefit 1: It gives wisdom, understanding and knowledge

Every day offers us an opportunity, through various experiences, to enrich our wealth of knowledge. The ability to apply this knowledge most beneficially to ourselves and our community can be considered wisdom.

The Bible uses the pronoun: "She" to describe wisdom. In it, she introduces herself to us in the book of Proverbs. She also gives solutions to his struggles and a guide to his actions. She shows that she is invaluable in all the decisions a man makes, like choosing a life partner, career path or even how and where to invest money. She maintains that her absence in the life of people can lead to death (Proverbs 10:21).

Even God Himself functions using wisdom (Proverbs 3:19). He possessed her first, and so should we. She is worth more than gold, and her benefits are worth more than the best treasures (Proverbs 8:19).

To activate the wisdom that we need to go through life, we must first learn to fear the Lord (Psalm 111:10). This fear influences every decision that we make through the consideration that one day we will be held to account for all our words and actions before a great God. It enables us to apply knowledge in a way devoid of evil.

Without the fear of the Lord, our actions will be more determined by emotions like hate and greed. We will become essentially self-seeking and devoid of empathy or the fear of accountability. The benefits of the concept of the fear of the Lord may not, at first instance, be understood. That is because of the power that it carries.

The Bible says that the fear of the Lord cannot be understood- until it is sought with desperate longing. I remember those comic books I used to love so much that told stories of treasure hunts and the many obstacles and treacheries that lay in the path of success. Many of those stories eventually ended up on our screens as great movies. I can still remember the desperate desires and self-motivation of the actors in them.

To understand the fear of the Lord, we must search for it like the desperate and determined characters in those treasure hunts, searching through maps of deserted islands and ready to dig as deep as is necessary to find what they sought (Proverbs 2:3-5). Consider the Bible as a map and the Holy Spirit as a compass. Hopefully, this book may serve as your straight edge as you place your "X" to mark the spot. Take the time to read through its pages and be determined to act. It is only by making wisdom part of your desperate search and by getting understanding that we can find the fear of the Lord.

Job in the Bible defined wisdom and went further to explain understanding. He said it was simply avoiding evil. I believe that a person whose conscience is active, will always take a minute to sift every intention through good moral judgement (Job 28:28).

Young persons who especially desire the Lord to be the   foundation of their generation and want to open the door to justice, righteousness, wisdom and knowledge must use a key known as the fear of the Lord (Isaiah 33:5-6 NIV).

Benefit 2: Gives long life

Researchers studying childhood trauma and brain development have found that Adverse Childhood

Experiences (ACEs), if allowed to be repeated and prolonged, have been discovered to lead to Toxic Stress that can, over time, significantly shorten the lifespan of children. This information was presented after studies and observation. (https://www.adversechildhoodexperiences.co.uk/aces).

Simply put, ACEs can cut short the lifespan of individuals if not well managed. Think about this for a while. Researchers are saying that besides natural occurrences like earthquakes, tsunamis and pandemics, lots of the man caused sources of shortened life spans, like drug abuse, crime, and gang membership, can be reduced by managing ACEs.

For young Christians, the fear of the Lord and the passing down from one generation to the next, His precepts, breaks the cycle of sin. Doing that also takes care of what these researchers refer to as ACEs. The outcome for all of us is peace, victory and prosperity.

The point here is that the fear of the Lord guides our decisions in obedience to the will of God, which in turn shapes our conduct and produces in us attitudes without future consequences that are negative.

Many historical accounts of the lives of people who lived evil lives proved that their lives were usually short and that they were also quickly forgotten. Therefore, to live long and healthy, we must develop the fear of the Lord (Proverbs 10:27).

Just one wrong decision can lead a young man into a death trap. When confronted with a need to make decisions such as whether to join a gang or a cult or find the easy way out through drugs, sex or crime, the fear of the Lord becomes an invaluable compass to making the right choice. That still small voice in you that says, "No, Come on!" Or "you are better than that" Usually originates from the fear of the Lord. The fear of the Lord keeps a young man alive and ensures that he does not die young (Proverbs 14:27).

Benefit 3: Gives divine-direction

One big challenge for many Christians to this day has been decision-making. Many of us find it difficult to make right choices, especially when we have destiny-impacting choices. When there are too many options, too much information and available options are elusive, it becomes difficult to choose.

Decisions like what career path to follow and who to marry require prayerful considerations. Making wrong choices in such situations can seriously distort destiny and believe it- that's precisely what the devil wants.

The selection of a life partner can be considered critical because whatever choice we make can leave the parties involved disoriented and shattered. For this reason, I strongly advise that this decision is taken with the guidance of the Holy Spirit, who will give peace to show His approval after desperate and fervent prayer to seek His counsel.

For people with the fear of the Lord, the path to follow is not always challenging. That is because the Lord Himself, sends directions. For instance, those in need of blessings like jobs, may receive it after years of searching, and it may eventually come in multiple offers from different sectors. They may also come with attractive packages that can leave the receiver confused and unable to decide which one to pick.

The best choice may not be the one with the fattest pay cheque, but the one the Holy Spirit leads them to pick after asking the Lord. Choosing without recourse to God in such matters would only lead to many bumps and bruises on their way. But those who fear the Lord will learn from Him in such situations the best pick (Psalm 25:12).

Benefit 4: Gives divine-protection

Many countries have citizens of high value that are specially protected. To be considered for such a privilege, certain criteria must be met and the necessary approvals given. Sometimes others around these high value citizens also benefit from these special arrangements. That was how God remembered Lot on account of Abraham (Genesis 19:29).

A very popular Nigerian pastor narrated a story in one of his services of a memorable flight experience. He recounted how the aeroplane he was travelling in experienced strong turbulence. While this went going on, many of the passengers on board exhibited vivid fear. In the midst of all of this, he heard one of the passengers tell another to calm down with the assurance that nothing would go wrong because a certain man of God was on-board, and surely God would deliver them on his account.

In security, there is a dichotomy between those who have the fear of the Lord and others. One of the divine duties usually assigned to angels by God is to ensure the safety of those that fear Him, just as the Chief Executive of any country approves special security arrangements for high-value citizens. These angels stick around very closely to ensure that no harm comes to such people in all circumstances. (Psalm 34:7).

Benefit 5: Gives riches

The ability to become rich comes from the Lord (Deuteronomy 8:18) if we make Him a part of our lives. Making him part of our lives requires that we live our daily lives with a conscious effort to please God. Young people who desire true riches must learn to live lives that please God first.

The principles of the fear of God should be practical for them to reap the benefit that it brings, which is the blessing of God. The fear of the Lord with a great deal of humility will surely make every desire to be rich a reality (Proverbs 22:4).

Benefit 6: Gives honour

Peter, (not his real name) served in our local church. He was always desirous of honour and complained so many times about how he deserved better recognition for his contributions to the smooth running of the church.

For some reason, he expected church members to compliment and show recognition of his efforts in the service of the Lord. Their supposed lack of recognition of his work seemed to be an encumbrance for him. But what he did not know was where honour comes. It comes from the fear of the Lord. Wherever honour for God is, His favour is usually not far away.

Finding favour with God and people is the exclusive reserve of those that fear the Lord, as communicated in a message to one of the early priests (Eli) whose sons had, in their actions, shown no fear for the Lord. He was told that God is interested in and honours those who honour Him. He sees their fear for Him. Honour usually stands close to riches, so those the Lord calls should serve in humility; they must obey him in every situation.

Benefit 7: God's friendship and access to secrets

The Lord makes friends with persons who honour Him and always makes and keeps His covenant with them as He did in the life of Abraham (Psalm 25:14).

Do you not draw your friends close? Do you not share your secrets, frustrations and plans with them? Certainly you will do all these things and even more, as God did in the life of Moses.

As for Abraham, did He not call him a friend (Isaiah 41:8) and greatly prosper him in addition to granting the deepest desire of his heart? Questions like this are supposed to stir up thoughts and steer them to the realization that there are great benefits if we befriend God- which can only be achieved by those who fear Him.

Benefit 8: Ensures answers to prayer

Prayer allows us to pour out our hearts to God. It provides a communication channel between Him and us. A popular hymn encourages us to pray if our paths are drear (SS&S 836).

One basic instinct of man when in trouble is to seek divine intervention. Many have prayed the simple prayer: "Lord, please help me!" With the hope that a negative situation would change. The reality that follows is that they don't always do, even for the most consistent churchgoer or most dedicated Chorister. Frustrating right? Why are the prayers of some people answered and those of others left unanswered?

A significant quantity of literature can be found on how to obtain answers to prayers. Jesus taught His disciples how to pray (Luke 11) and the Bible also captures instances when He took time out to pray (Mark 1:35 & Luke 6:12). So, the fact that we ought to pray continuously is not in doubt, but what we must strive for is to get answers each time we pray. One of the ways to measures a successful prayer life is when we consistently receive answers.

To have a successful prayer life, we are encouraged to pray with a humble and God-fearing heart, following the example of Jesus, who offered up prayers and petitions with fervent cries and tears, and was always heard. I mean, His prayers were always answered. The reason for this, was because He feared God (Hebrews 5:7 NKJV).

Can you remember our description of the spirit of the fear of the Lord? When this spirit comes upon a man, it distinguishes him; even his prayers go out with power. Joseph had this spirit, it gave him wisdom, and favour and eventually led him from the prison to the palace (Genesis 37). The fear of the Lord can do the same for us today- it can get us away from our challenges, then, like a catapult-like thrust, seats us among kings.

CHAPTER 3
Gaining Wisdom

"A wise man may look ridiculous in the company of fools"
-                    *Thomas Fuller*

Show me a person without wisdom, and I, with certainty, can predict that the future of such a person will be one filled with guilt and regret. The reason is that wisdom ensures that we fulfil God's purpose for our lives here on earth by guiding our choices to joy and prosperity.

Now, many people believe that wisdom is the application of knowledge gathered over time. Whether we gain this knowledge through suffering or sound teaching, what is important is our ability to appropriately apply whatever insight we gain through experience or instruction in our everyday lives.

I had strived to gather knowledge beyond my university degrees and developed a keen interest in wealth creation. I realised early in my life the power of networking and the stock market and started gathering as much knowledge as I could absorb. So there I was, with my meagre earned income and tonnes of information needed for an early start at trying to build residual income.

In retrospect, I also realised that the most pertinent knowledge and the first that I should have sought was the existence of God and His power to make me succeed. It would have guided my decisions and preserved my increase.

Knowing God exposes us to His expectations of us. When we begin to strive toward meeting these expectations, we begin to build wisdom. God expects us to love, obey and reverently fear Him. Jesus teaches that if we love Him, we ought to obey Him. Respectfully doing this is where our journey to wisdom begins.

It became clear to me that the power gained through knowing God first is so profound, so much so that over time, I observed its ability to act as a magnet and how it attracts all the other things we need. When we run after the kingdom, the other things that we need (job, marriage, car etc.) are attracted to us. They, in turn, run after us. The likelihood that we will find the kingdom when we seek it is in the assurance that God, in his word, assures us of His delight to give us this kingdom whenever we seek it (Luke 12:32).

To fear the Lord means to obey Him. Therefore, an attempt to remain on the path of wisdom involves developing a desire to find out and do what God wants to be done in every situation. That reflects the understanding that His will is a key to achieving our purpose here on earth (Ephesians 5:17). Knowing the mind of God on every matter is very important in our walk of glory.

God knows the heart of all people. He knows those that are willing to obey Him and those that are not. We must strive to know Him incrementally by drawing nearer and doing what He says one at a time to achieve our purpose and a life of glory (Act 13:22).

To achieve obedience, we must detach ourselves from many things that distract us and prevent our hearts from following what is most beneficial. We need to break away from whatever takes our focus from God (Romans 12:2).

Honestly, this requires a lot of discipline because, as they say, "The world is ever near us". So, how we use our time is pertinent. That includes what we watch on television and mobile devices, where we go, who we associate with and most importantly, how we behave. Our time spent thinking must be about how to please God and not how to run off to do evil.

After the development of reverential fear for the Lord, the next thing to do is cultivate a lifestyle of total obedience (Ecclesiastes 12:13). King David was always willing to obey God. It led to his being called a man after God's heart- who was willing to obey God in everything (Acts 13:22). Everything? Yes, everything. We ought to obey God in every situation. God is still looking for people like David, clearly showing the importance of obedience to Him.

The only way to know if we are obedient to God is if we regularly search out His word and make up our minds to do what it says. King David of Israel once wrote about hiding the word of God in his heart. And Jeremy Brummel wrote about how to obey it in a song sung as a marching song by primary school pupils all over Nigeria. It goes this way:

> "Obedience is the very best way to show that you believe
> Doing exactly what the Lord commands and doing it happily
> Action is the key do it immediately joy you will receive
> Obedience is the very best way to show that you believe
> O-B-E-D-I-E-N-C-E. Obedience is the very best way to show that you believe"

One way to motivate yourself to do what God wants you to do happily is to fill your heart with gratitude. This process may involve many other actions that are very helpful in getting you to that point of gratefulness. Think back at what He has done in your life- however small. Remember that He gave up His life on the cross so you can have life. Look around you and see what He has done in the life of others, and allow your heart to fill with great expectation that He can do the same and even more for you. He can help you achieve whatever transformation you need in life.

There is great power in serving the Lord. Service must be taken very seriously. When we unpack what it means to serve God, doesn't it still point to obedience? That is why even before going into whatever form of service, it is wise to have worked on ourselves to develop a willing heart to obey God in all situations.

It is erroneous to ask God to bless us first before we serve Him. I remember one brother, like many others before him, who was going through hard times, and we asked to come closer to the Lord to receive a solution. He told us that if God wanted his service, He should bless him first. The truth is that it does not work that way. We should first do God's work in faith, and while we are at it, He becomes pleased to begin to do ours.

GOD REWARDS OBEDIENCE

Jesus speaks about the two great commandments that all have to do with love in the twenty-second chapter of the book of Matthew. God demonstrated His love for the world by giving His only begotten son to hang on a tree and die for it. Love here is more than a feeling of affection for someone but runs deeper. It is a sincere decision of the will to be committed to a person beyond mere words.

Now that same God wants us to follow His example and be committed to Him through a love that proceeds from the depth of our hearts, soul and mind (Mathew 22:37).

God loves us. He gave what was priceless to prove this love and now demands reciprocity. He wants us to be willing to give whatever we consider priceless just as He was willing to do the same for us. The best way to demonstrate this willingness is to do whatever He says. Abraham demonstrated it through his willingness to sacrifice his beloved Isaac to Jehovah. God saw his heart and the action he took in obedience and recorded how He became convinced that Abraham honoured and feared Him (Genesis 22:12 GNT).

It is normal to want to please persons that we love, and in God's case, He wants us to do this by obeying Him (John 14:15).

Obedience draws us closer to God. It connects us. Disobedience, on the other hand, can lead us away from His presence and bring curses or even death.

Adam and Eve were given instructions by God, whom they knew very well, yet went ahead to act in disobedience. That led them to hide from God and eventually banished from the Garden of Eden with a few curses as "Jara" (meaning, in addition).

A young prophet was charged with an important task to achieve in a town. He was given strict instructions not to make stops on the road and not to eat while on this important assignment and expected to take his assignment seriously by quickly getting it done without being distracted. The reasons for his instructions were best known to the one who sent him.

He disobeyed these instructions after listening to the deception of an older prophet. It led to the pronouncement of judgement on him through the mouth of that same older prophet- the one who got him into trouble in the first place.

The world is full of lies and distractions, but that is no excuse for outright disobedience to God. We must trust "The Almighty" when it comes to the things that He says and avoid getting misled. They might tell you just how experienced they are or even how harmless or beneficial your disobedience may be, but you must take the initiative to stay the course and refuse to yield to their deceptions.

Obedience has rewards that far outweigh whatever benefit we may gain from rebellion. They are numerous and can impact our journey to victory powerfully. These fifteen rewards, observed in the lives of people who obeyed God, have been compiled. I am sure that there are many others that you may feel like adding to the list. Please do. Meanwhile, let us get started with these:

Reward 1: Obedience makes us God's friends

It's not hard to understand why God describes His servants Abraham and Moses as friends. They all had something in common- righteousness. They were men who were committed to obeying God.

Jesus, talking to his disciples about friendship, speaks about how instead of calling us servants, He calls us friends. What an upgrade! But note; this offer is only available to the obedient among us. (John 15:14).

Reward 2: Obedience brings revelation

Revelation is the disclosure of spiritual truths by divine or supernatural release. Only those who obey the Lord receive revelation. (Deuteronomy 29:29).

God is always ready to share insights, but He only does this with obedient servants. They are the ones who believe and trust. They can be trusted to pursue and act as instructed when revelation comes.

Reward 3: Obedience brings righteousness

Our obedience can trigger righteousness in others. Considering the life of Jesus, this is very practicable in church governance, where the obedience of leaders can influence the followership.

That is not just because their actions are examples but because the divine power to unlock blessings and the spirit of the fear of the Lord is released (Romans 5:19).

Reward 4: Obedience qualifies us for the Holy Spirit

After receiving God's message to repentance and being baptised in the name of our triune God, we become ready to receive the Holy Spirit.

The Holy Spirit, who also with ours bears witness to our being children of God, is not just given to anybody by the Lord. He is gifted to those who live in constant obedience to God (Act 5:32).

Reward 5: Obedience makes us God's favourites

Every parent potentially has a thing for that child that displays the character of obedience. In local Nigerian settings, a father may even be heard laying claim to such a child.

Who says that God has no favourites? It might be worth noting that there is a difference between obedient and disobedient children of God, and the obedient ones among us are His favourites. They always get what they ask. God gives them the best.

That is so because the earth belongs to the Lord, including every one of us but those of us who are obedient, are special- a status that qualifies us to be able to approach our father whenever we like and assures us that He will give the attention we need (Exodus 19:5).

Reward 6: Obedience brings promotion

Promotion does not come from the east or the west but from the Lord (Psalm 75:6-7), who rewards those He chooses by promoting them. Joseph, in the Bible's book of Genesis, through continuous obedience, was promoted to a position that made him the number two man in Egypt.

He was a man who suffered betrayal by his brothers, slavery in Egypt, a false accusation that landed him in prison and disappointment by the king's Cup Bearer, whom he expected help from- perhaps a good word to the king or something of the sort, to get him out of prison. Despite these, he remained obedient to the God his father taught him to honour.

If we remain obedient despite whatever situation we may be in, we will surely end up like Joseph. The Lord promotes His obedient and loyal children.

Reward 7: Obedience leads to greatness

Obedience puts a distinction on us and in this distinction, we become greater than our peers. It is the key to greatness, showing that God is still interested in those ready to obey Him in all situations. He made that promise long ago and it still stands (Deuteronomy 28:1).

Reward 8: Obedience makes us blessed

Obeying God makes us prosper in whatever we do. It also makes us happy and admired by those around us. When we are blessed, it is difficult to hide it. The day a blessed man decides to invest in the stock market, the prices begin to change to his benefit, and even if he decides to sell water, the business does well.

Obeying God's word puts us in a position where we receive divine secrets for excellence like Joseph (Genesis 11), and failure becomes a thing of the past.

The happiness that follows the absence of failure due to obedience is what Jesus describes in the book of Luke (Luke 11:28). So, we must ensure that we are more than just hearers of the word but those that obey and practice it (James 1:25).

Reward 9: Obedience gives us victory

Remember that the Lord, who can see the hearts of all men, has His eyes running to and fro throughout the whole earth, looking for people whose hearts are right with Him so that He can manifest Himself on their behalf (2 Chronicles 16:9).

I see the word "Manifest" As the release of divine power to deliver victory to such people. For those struggling to get out of wilderness experiences and have to also contend with attacks from enemies "Within". Be strong! Let your heart be at peace by your understanding that the God you serve fights for you

Moses told the Israelites they would not have to do anything because God would fight for them. That is because when we remain obedient to God, our enemies become His and our adversaries, His too (Exodus 23:22 NIV).

Have you ever heard that the LORD, The Lion of the Tribe of Judah, Jehovah, lost a battle? If He has not and is not likely to ever lose. He also promises to take up all our enemies, which means that we can be sure of being victorious at all times. He deals with all those who oppose us.

Reward 10: Obedience brings prosperity

Once, a dying king told his son a secret, one that had guided him all his life. This secret was meant to ensure that this young and inexperienced soon-to-be-king and son of his, would be successful in everything he did and it was also intended to ensure that the throne was preserved.

What was this secret? It was to be obedient to God (I kings 2:3). The king made his son understand that if he stayed obedient to the Lord, he would prosper in whatever he did. This principle has not changed. The secret to true success is not in how connected we are, or in our antecedence but in living a life of total obedience to the word of God. (Joshua 1:8).

You see, God has a plan for each of us. He wants us to have the kind of future we dream of (Jeremiah 29:11), but we must realise that He is the source of everything. We have; because He gives, and we are; because He makes. He owns that future we seek, and He alone can guide us there.

Therefore, obedience is key. It is very subjective. So if we agree to serve God and be obedient to His word, we can be sure that we shall end our days in prosperity, and when we take stock of our lives at the end of it, it will be clear that we are blessed (Job 36:11).

Reward 11: Obedience brings restoration

Restoration may be needed in our marriage, family, health, career, ministry, business and the list goes on and on. Learning to trust and obey the word of God draws to us whatever type of restoration we desire.

A woman known as the "Shunammite woman" Was warned of an impending famine by a man of God known as Elisha. He asked her to leave home to escape the disaster, and she obeyed.

She went to live in the land of the Philistines for seven years and returned to great favour and blessings from the Lord. (II kings 8:2). This was all because she obeyed the man of God. Even though at some point, she ran into some challenges like we always do, in the end, she experienced restoration.

God is always speaking to us in various ways, so we must always be ready. Even when it seems our actions put us in a difficult situation, we must still hope to hear from Him. That is because the Lord can restore whatever we lose in time, money and material.

Reward 12: Obedience brings favour

Favour is the Lord's reward for obedience. He told the first king of Israel- Saul, through a prophet known as Samuel, that obedience was better than sacrifice (I Samuel 15:22).

The point is that obedience which shows that we trust and honour God pleases Him much more than whatever kind of mundane plan we feel like putting together. The point here is when God tells us to do something, exactly what He says should be what we do.

Saul, who was highly favoured and chosen as the first king of Israel, was subsequently rejected by the Lord as king. To replace him, David- a young man with the heart to obey God in everything, who attracted favour from God, was chosen.

Reward 13: Obedience brings long life

There is a secret to long life, which is obedience. Just like children who obey their parents are rewarded with a long life by God, we, who are children of God also, will be rewarded with long lives if we obey Him.

The Bible tells us about Enoch, the father of Methuselah, who lived 365 years and pleased God so much that he was not allowed to die but was taken by God (Hebrews 11:5).

Can you now see the relationship between obedience and long life? There is great power in being obedient to God, and this power, also ensures that we exceed expectations in all we do, depending on what the father wants.

So, in addition to whatever modern exercise, rest, diet or social interaction techniques we learn and practice, let us add obedience. It works!

Reward 14: Obedience brings further instructions

Prophecy comes in incomplete packages for reasons best known to the Holy Spirit. Though that is because he likes first things first, it is also because by doing so, He can gently guide us into obedience and protect us too.

Prophecy must come with a solution, like an instruction from God that we ought to follow for victory.

Without obeying the first set of instructions, the Holy Spirit may not give more on a matter.

In the case of Abraham, the Lord spoke to him, telling him to leave his father's country to a place he would be directed. Until he obeyed that first instruction, the Lord did not make any covenant with him. The more he obeyed, the more he received new instructions (Genesis 12).

Phillip in the Bible was instructed by the Holy Spirit to travel on the road that led to Gaza. He did not know what exactly he was to do there but obeyed. It was after he had obeyed, he received further instructions (Acts 8).

Reverend Imeh Ukpong once told a story about how the Holy Spirit instructed him to dress up and catch a bus with no particular destination in mind. He did and found himself travelling with an old acquaintance who had been searching for him unsuccessfully for a while.

Well, at the end of the meeting, the reverend had received financial support from his acquaintance because he obeyed the instruction of the Holy Spirit. When God speaks, speedily do what He says.

Reward 15: Obedience brings the answer to prayer

Since obedience is doing the will of God, and He is pleased when we obey Him, He says to us that we will receive whatever we ask Him for (1 John 3:22 NIV).

Living in disobedience is a sin that prevents our prayers from being answered (John 9:31).

All the devil needs to do is arrange a situation that places a child of God in disobedience and then quickly act against the prayers of that child.

These days, it is easy to find many young people who have no interest in God and have no use for His word. They lose interest when the word of God is preached and they go ahead and live as they like. They fornicate, tattoo their bodies and speak guile. They speak evil of respectable men of God publicly on social media and cause trouble. The prayers of such people will not receive answers unless they are praying prayers of repentance (Proverbs 28:19).

If ever we fall into sudden trouble, our obedience guarantees that when we call to the Lord, He will answer (Jeremiah 33:3).

Being a Christian does not mean that you will not have challenges or troubles in your life but what you can be sure of is that the force to overcome is available. Also, if you ever face sudden calamity and cry out to the Lord, He will surely answer.

I have heard of people who have had experiences like robberies, car crashes and so on and who cried out in distress and received miraculous responses from the Lord. These testimonies are very common in the lives of God's obedient children. Concerning the disobedient, they do not enjoy such privileges. When they call, if ever in trouble, their sins stand in the way (Psalm 1:28).

HOW TO OBEY GOD

Obedience can be very challenging, especially when it is not done out of love. There is always one reason why our obedience cannot be complete; always one thing we want to accomplish rather than obeying God.

It helps to realise that whatever we have was only given to us as caretakers by God, who always has plans for us that are beyond our imaginations.

Also, difficulties, challenges and sufferings may be our experience for a while, but we must understand that they won't last and are meant to take us to our destinies, just like serving in prison and in Potipher's house where leadership training experiences for Joseph. Experiences he could not have gotten at home. Suffering teaches us humility and helps us in our obedience walk.

In many instances, tough times draw us closer to the Lord, and we end up thankful. Obedience is a class that we must take in the school of our Christian transformation, it is one that even our Lord Jesus took (Hebrews 5:8).

I have put together a few suggestions to build an obedient character. It has worked for many Christians and can work for you too. Though these may not be the only ways to become obedient to God, we ought to apply them and depend on the Holy Spirit to guide us to what extra things to do.

Constant prayer

Pouring our hearts out to the Lord in prayer and asking him to help our love walk is the first step. Many Christians have testified to the efficacy of this.

Invite the Holy Spirit to teach you the things you need to know while on your journey and strengthen and reform you. The power released at the altar of prayer can transform lives.

Reading the Bible every day

Could there be a better way to know about God other than by reading the story of how He created the world in the very beginning and how much He loves us and gave up His only son for us? The stories in this Holy Spirit-inspired book can change our lives forever.

Resolutions

That often follows the realisation that God loves us so much. We can decide to commit ourselves to a life that responds to this love through a resolution to avoid certain things and just be obedient to His word.

A tribe, in response to the Lord, decided never to drink alcohol. Their decision passed to every generation, was recorded in the Bible. This tribe was called the Rechabites. (Jeremiah 35)

Consider the above rewards for obedience

This strategy involves a review of all the benefits of being obedient. Everyone knows that a system that promotes reward; can be more effective than one that promotes punishment.

Man has discovered that rewards have been much more effective than punishment. These rewards should be no exception. The most prominent benefit of obedience is the reward of eternal life. The fore-mentioned rewards are just additions.

CHAPTER 4
The Robber Has No Honour

"As snow in summer, and as rain in harvest, so honour is not seemly for a fool"
- *King Solomon*

In recent times, there has been so much controversy surrounding tithing. Church podiums and social media platforms have been awash with debates on the relevance and necessity of tithing. Participants in these debates have put up all sorts of arguments and messages in support of their views.

Giving must never be a daunting task or a compulsory burden but an opportunity for a blessing because it opens the door to divine supply. A closed palm, they say, can only retain its content; it cannot receive more.

The arguments in these debates isolate three views on tithing. The first view is that there is nothing wrong with tithing as currently practised. Christians obey God by honouring Him with ten per cent (10%) of their income, and for this, they get blessed. It's that simple.

The second view is held by those who believe that the payment of tithe is an Old Testament law requirement and not relevant in the New Covenant. They argue that there is nowhere in the New Testament where followers of Jesus are encouraged to pay tithe in a legalistic system. Instead, they were encouraged to give gifts, as captured in 1 Corinthians 16:2.

The third view holds that paying tithes, as is currently practised, restricts giving to just ten per cent (10%) of our increase, whereas Christians should be allowed as much of tithes as they can afford, even if what they paid is in deficit or excess of this percentage. That means that some may give seven per cent (7%), while others can pay tithes as much as forty per cent (40%), based on whatever they decide in their hearts (2 Corinthians 9:7).

The belief here is that such people are dead to the law and should not be under any obligation but should be allowed to give in proportion to their wills and sacrificially also. They feel that church leaders should not enforce or monitor their giving (1 Corinthians 16:1-2).

The third group's view has no faith in the practice of systematic tithing and distrusts the system responsible for managing their tithes. For them, it is preferable to use whatever people pay to help the poor and needy than to send them to the church. That, to them, makes more sense because they feel that the church doesn't do enough for the poor and believe that more can be done for them with tithes rather than grow ministries that ignore their plight.

I know that many people share one or more of these views. As for me, the third view used to appeal to me. Firstly because the first view seemed like I could not differentiate between tithing and philanthropy and secondly because I hadn't sound knowledge, commitment and faith. I will like to share my experience, including what the Holy Spirit told me about paying my tithe.

At one time, I became very critical of what churches did with my tithe. So I would tell those who cared to listen at the time that I was a believer in responsible giving – a principle I described as being in use when I take up the responsibility of ensuring that the money I pay as tithe is managed in an accountable and targeted manner.

At another time, after reading one of the Bible portions used to drive the second view about tithing and listening to a couple of teachings that discouraged tithing, I decided that it was the biggest deception in modern Christianity. I also believed that tithe paying had no place in the New Covenant that Christians shared in Christ Jesus. I was wrong.

The truth was that I was struggling with paying my tithe and needed one good reason not to. You see, telling people not to participate in the tithing covenant is a deliberate attempt, as I view it, to provide a contract for such people to sign into poverty. For years I did not pay tithe.

The money just never seemed enough, no matter how much I had. I had even gotten irritated that churches outrightly spoke about paying a tenth and stopped attending church. This decision was followed by more hardship. It was as though heaven's supply windows were solidly shut against me, and I began to slide deeper into the pool of lack. By the time I realised my situation, I no longer had an income from which I could pay my tithe.

Then one day, the Holy Spirit spoke to me in church during one of our meetings known as the Spiritual Convention. He promised to help me. He told me very clearly that what I ought to do first was to start paying my tithe. In my heart, I was confused and would have asked Him how that was possible considering my lack of income, but I just obeyed.

I began to tithe even without a job and was willing and determined to obey the Holy Spirit and become faithful in little. I never once looked back since then and will share much of the knowledge that informed my decision.

You may also hear from the Holy Spirit like I did, in addition to what you are about to read, but the bottom line is that the tithing as a covenant is one of the kingdom strategies that keep God's children out of lack.

WHAT DOES THE LORD SAY ABOUT TITHING?

Many people view tithing as a method of taxation to provide for the needs of the priests and Levites in the Old Testament times. They are under the illusion that pastors nowadays are under a different law and not subject to such provisions. That view is incorrect.

Tithing is an Old Testament concept which required that the Israelites bring to the temple ten per cent (10%) of everything that they produced, like the crops they grew and the livestock they raised in all the land (Leviticus 27:30 & 2 Chronicles 31:5).

One Bible passage that used to be a challenge for many to deal with, as regards tithing, including me, is Deuteronomy 14:24, which talks about how we should spend a tenth of our earnings and what to do if the temple is far away. This passage also encourages us to remember our responsibilities to priests, widows and orphans, which entails we pay a tenth of our increase into the Lord's temple.

The Lord had also reprimanded His children on paying their tithes by asking them, through one of His prophets, if it was right for people to rob God. They asked Him how this was possible, and He explained that they had refused to pay tithes and offerings.

One Bible translation described the refusal of the children of God to pay tithe using the word "Cheat". The reason is that not paying their tithe can be likened to cheating God (Malachi 3:8). Another used the word "Rob" Which makes sense since everything belongs to God-who gives to man out of His abundance. Therefore when we take what has not been given by God, we rob Him. I can even hilariously assume that the non-tithe payer who owns a car rides around in stolen property.

HAS GOD'S POSITION ON TITHE CHANGED?

The answer to this question is "No". You see we are prone to changes in our character, fundamental beliefs and judgements.

God is not like us. He tells a little about His character- about how He's not flaky, to change what He expects from His children, or what He says He would do for them (Malachi 3:6).

Who should pay tithe?

We now know that not paying tithe in the scriptures is robbery. I know many churches where even leaders do not pay their tithes. Oh! How dangerous this is. Firstly because it is a bad example for their followers, and secondly because such an attitude can bring poverty to these leaders.

The blessings that tithing brings are for every child of God. In the Old Testament, even the Levites paid tithes to Aaron. (Numbers 18:26).

TITHING IS A COVENANT

A covenant is a willful and binding solemn agreement between two or more individuals. It is usually used in religious language to describe agreements between God and us - an agreement to do something.

Tithe, which refers to a tenth, was first given by our father Abraham to Melchizedek, the king of Salem and priest of the Highest God (Genesis 14:18-20,) and it is a covenant in the sense that if we tithe, we immediately have access to God's promises concerning tithing (Malachi 3:10)

Tithing has financial blessings tied to it, and like many people, what I previously did not realise, was that it was also an opportunity to sow. Our tithes are seeds that cannot fail to germinate into a harvest, following the law of sowing and reaping upon the earth (Genesis 8:22).

Christians who want to be blessed should tithe. Let no one deceive you that tithing is irrelevant in the church today. Remember that Jesus did not come to abolish the law but to fulfil it.

Tithing honours God and shows that we realise that He is the giver of wealth (Deuteronomy 8:18). Yes! God, Himself is a giver. He gave His only begotten son because of His love for the world. Christ expects us to love God with all our hearts, soul and mind. With such love, our giving does not just prove our love but honours Him too (Proverbs 3:9-10).

The covenant of tithing is entered into by choice and through faith. We must realise that God's promises, plus our faith lead to the miraculous, and in many cases, financial ones. Let us engage in tithing through faith-without which we cannot please God. By faith, we must give- believing that we also instantly receive the reward for our obedient giving.

BENEFITS OF TITHING

People who tithe do not struggle financially. The Lord keeps His promises to them. As I stated earlier, I used to be one of many the viewed tithing as an excessive burden. I never liked discussions about tithing. It was a topic that would make me change a television channel if it was going on. I had made up my mind that it was not necessary, and that was it. I guess you know the result- I was never financially stable.

Tithing also guarantees a supernatural supply. My pastor narrated how he earned one of his quick promotions. He spoke about how tieing our faith to our tithe can attract the miraculous. You see, what he did was to increase his tithe by faith, and that earned him a promotion. The thing was that spiritually, he had moved to a higher income immediately after he increased his tithe, and since the spiritual controls the physical, there was a physical manifestation.

One of the prominent scriptures referred to in discussions about tithing is Malachi 3:10. It will be our reference scripture, which we shall turn to and see what blessings are in store for tithe payers. These blessings gotten when we tithe are ours to claim by faith as long as we keep our part of the covenant in tithing.

The blessing of honour

God has integrity. What He says, He does. He promises to honour us among our counterparts if we honour Him (1 Samuel 2:30). You see, tithing is a practice that was started by Abraham and designed to bring honour to God. If we call ourselves children of God, our father expects to be honoured by us (Malachi 1:6).

God is not bothered about how much more of our income we give when we decide to. It is not about the sum of money we pay but the willingness to part with our ten per cent (10%) to honour Him, even if it adds up, in the end, to just a token.

So, forget about that plan to give Him fifty per cent (50%) in two months, just honour Him today with ten per cent (10%) and see if He won't honour you too.

The blessing of open floodgates of heaven

That is the first thing that we experience when we become covenant tithers. The opening of heaven's floodgates refers to a supernatural release. When heaven opens up its floodgates to a man, that man begins to experience breakthroughs. Opportunities begin to follow such a man, and dryness disappears.

The outpouring of God's blessings

Those who do not tithe are under a curse (Malachi 3:9 KJV), but those who keep God's ordinances enjoy its rewards.

Giving in God's honour shows our love for Him and attracts His blessing. The scripture above captures God's promise to tithers in the form of blessings too numerous to count.

To better understand this, imagine having so much of something, with friends and neighbours though benefiting, envious of your happiness and contentment. When God promises a person who tithes blessings, nobody can accurately predict the enormity or form it will take. Even the greatest minds cannot accurately predict God's plans. The blessings from the payment of tithes make people rich and successful in all endeavours.

The prevention of crop damage by pests and premature dropping of fruits in your vineyard

The Lord, by Himself, drives away whatever can distort or destroy the plans of any of His obedient children who tithes. Such a person's plans are always successful, with constant protection over whatever is the person's source of income.

Many people sow and never reap, but this is different with tithers. Their investments are always secure, and their financial expectations are always successful. When robbers and destruction seek victims, their navigation takes them away from those that tithe. That is all because the Lord watches over the affairs of such persons.

The blessing of being called blessed for yours will be a delightful land

The blessings that come upon those who tithe are usually so obvious to others far and wide that they begin to talk about how happy and prosperous they have become.

It is difficult to hide blessings that come through faithful tithing. That is not just because these blessings flow from heaven as a flood but also because they are unquantifiable, noticeable and worthy of envy.

CHAPTER 5
Power in Service

"He profits most who serves best."
-        *Arthur F. Sheldon*

My walk with the Lord has been a very educative experience. In retrospect, it promotes a compelling need to record a few observations and experience-triggered thoughts. I know many people who, through service, have received their long-awaited and desired miracles and can testify that God rewards service. Our service to the Lord must not be the kind done haphazardly. A word that should best qualify our service to God and which causes a release of His power is: "Wholehearted".

Wholehearted service is the kind of service that meets God's standards. It is the kind of service through which we can draw benefits. I have seen the barren receive miraculous babies because they decided to ignore their conditions and wholeheartedly serve God.

I have seen the jobless get miraculous employment, singles enter into loving and heaven-ordained marriages, healing from stubborn sicknesses, Secondary School leavers get admissions into universities to continue their studies, and the list goes on and on.

When our service meets God's standard, it proves we have faith in Him. God watches over our service, knows the hearts of all of us and knows who does or does not meet His standard of wholehearted service. As a reward, He pours out His power into the lives of his servants that measure up.

Caleb stood out. He was famed for his wholehearted service to God. That led to a record of his name and story included in the greatest book ever written (the Bible)

I realised that the quality of our service also qualifies us divinely. That was why Caleb was singled out by the Lord as the only person, in his time, to enter the Promised Land. That kind of favour is a generational blessing. And as in the case of Caleb, blessings like those are enjoyed by all our descendants (Deuteronomy 1:36).

THE CONCEPT OF SERVICE TO GOD

The concept of serving God dates back to the Old Testament. Its purpose is to glorify God, and it is compulsorily driven by reverence, love and the desire to be obedient to Him.

Joshua, before his death, urged the children of Israel to fear the Lord and serve Him. He publicly revealed the decision he and his family had taken concerning serving God (Joshua 24:14- 15).

The children of Israel witnessed the awesome power of God and His favour which delivered them from their bitter slavery in Egypt, with plunder, as payment for their years of hard labour. At the time of their deliverance, the Lord split the red sea for them and destroyed the army of Egypt with his mighty hand. The Israelites also enjoyed rivers in the desert, manna and quail, and were given cities they did not build in addition to vineyards they did not plant.

They should have, after all, that God had done for them, realised His superiority over other gods. He who called Himself "I am" Had through these acts, shown Himself greater than the Gods of Egypt and other worthless idols.

What Joshua expected from the Israelites, which is still an expectation from us today, was to submit to God in reverence and love. Such a submission ought to be done in a way that glorifies Him. Love in this context must be considered in its verb form as an emotion which needs to be expressed.

When the Pharisees tested Jesus, He explained that the first and greatest commandment is love. He said, "Love the Lord your God with all your heart and with all your soul and with all your mind" (Mathew 22:37).

When we love, we are always willing to serve, and faithfully too. Therefore, the proof of love for God can best be expressed in the quality of our reverential service to Him.

THE SERVICE STANDARD

To serve God requires that we fulfil some expected duties to Him. These duties are to fear Him and obey His commandments (Ecclesiastes 12:13). Suffice is to say, to serve God is to reverentially obey Him.

Knowing that Jesus says that if we love Him, we should obey him. The proof of our love for God must be our obedience to His commandments (John 14:15-21). He exemplified true love by seeking to accomplish the will of His father. Even when He knew that obeying His father meant death, albeit a horrifying one on the cross, He still yielded.

As stated earlier, God searches for persons willing to obey Him in all circumstances as proof of their love for Him and Jesus throughout His ministry, demonstrated this through total obedience. He is an example of service to God.

As Jesus prepared to wash the feet of His disciples, He taught them about true service. He told them how the Son of Man came, not to be served, but to serve and give His life as a ransom for others (Mark 10:45). Washing their feet was a practical show of love and humility - an example we ought to follow in our service to each other (John 13:1-17).

ACCEPTABLE SERVICE

We were all created to serve and worship God, but not all service meets God's righteous standard. I realised just how easy it was to serve, or improve on service to God if I first learned obedience.

For me, I saw a connection between obedience, zeal and Acceptable service. I also realised, after reading the Bible, that man has limited insight and can only see outward appearances and actions. God on the other hand, has unlimited insights and the ability to not just see outward actions, but inward thoughts too. That means deep into the heart of all of us.

That, therefore, means that nothing is hidden from Him, including the state and intention of our hearts while we serve. It also makes it important for those of us who serve or intend to serve, to do so with the right mindset, attitude and intention. This mindset controls our service and pushes service beyond trying to be in vogue or please others.

God is looking for people who will serve Him with zeal. He is looking for men and women with the right kind of hearts willing to zealously serve. David expressed this zeal for God's house as one that was consuming (Psalm 69:9).

Whatever is pleasing and acceptable to God is usually in line with His word. That is the reason why obedience, zeal and Acceptable service are all interwoven.

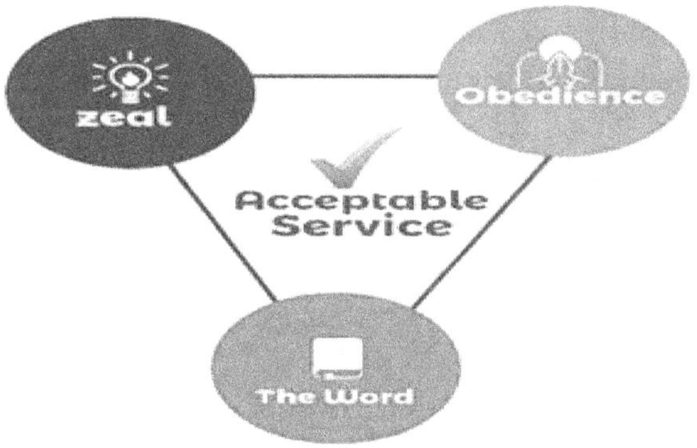

Components of Acceptable Service

The kind of service we offer to God comes with rewards or consequences. I took time to examine the type of service King David offered to the Lord (Acts 13:36) and how he was rewarded. I then went further to compare David's service to those offered by the sons of Aaron, the priest (Leviticus 10:1-3) and Uzzah, who drove the cart used to transport the Ark of Covenant back from the land of the Philistines (2 Samuel 6:7).

Consider the life of David, who was the least among his brothers but was chosen by God to be King over Israel. God Himself, called David a man after His own heart and spoke about him in the Bible much more than any other man after Jesus. There were about 971 mentions of David's name across various translations. The biggest reward I see in being a man like David is the glory and blessing that God's approval brings into our lives (Exodus 23:25).

The sons of Aaron, a priest in the Bible, were Nadab and Abihu. They were also priests, who one day took their censers and put fire in them, then added incense. They offered illegal fires before the Lord, which was against the His command. The consequence of their action was a fire from the Lord that led to their deaths. I see this as a lesson to pastors such as myself. We should avoid illegal assignments and services outside God's commandments and church regulations.

The need to apply the principles of Acceptable service cannot be overemphasized. As I reviewed other Bible passages, it was clear that serving God haphazardly brought death, many of which were sudden (Jeremiah 48:10).

The story of Uzzah, one of the sons of Abinadab who served God with his brother Ahio, is another one that also showed how God deals with unacceptable service. Uzzah, while carrying out his service, failed to show reverence for the Ark and his life taken by God suddenly. He may have become too familiar with the box and did not acknowledge its holiness, which angered God.

Again, I wondered how many of us have become too familiar with God and forgotten how holy He is while serving Him. I knew that God was willing to, by His mighty hand, remove whatever obstacle would stand in the way of my service to Him and that He was giving instructions to my captors, just as He did to the pharaoh, ordering the release of the children of Israel (Exodus 8:1 and 4:22-23).

PRINCIPLES OF ACCEPTABLE SERVICE TO GOD

A review of the attitude of the Israelites when they eventually received God's guidance or service manual throws a lot of light on the concept of Acceptable service to Him. Those actions taken by the children of Israel, which stirred up God's anger and judgment, must be avoided at all costs if we intend to serve Him acceptably.

For me, putting the desert experience in the Bible was meant to enrich this topic. I am sure that we will certainly find it useful in developing our acceptable service principles. Consider these:

Serve God without complaining, grumbling, whining, griping and murmuring

God dislikes it when we begin to grumble, whine, gripe and complain right in the middle of a process. He made it very clear to the children of Israel that whenever they complained and grumbled, it was not against leaders like Moses and Aaron but against Him.

Their attitude showed that they did not trust God and were ungrateful. The children of Israel, along with two hundred and fifty (250) other people, rebelled against Moses (Numbers 16:2), and Miriam and Aaron at one point also rebelliously questioned the leadership of Moses (Numbers 12).

Instead of grumbles and murmurs, like was done against Moses and Aaron (Exodus 16), leaders are to be respected. Remember that nobody can become a leader without the permission of God.

Complaining, whining, griping and murmuring do not encourage our leaders in any way. Instead, they irritate and in many cases, even infuriate them. It also infuriates the God that appointed them. A better option is to pray for them while we continue to support them as much as possible (1 Timothy 2:2).

Serve God with obedience to His word

The most required quality for anybody who wants to serve God is an obedient heart. Obeying the word of God gives life. The Israelites defied God by rejecting His commands. That was unacceptable by God's service standard (Ezekiel 20:18, 20 - 21, 23 - 24).

There are two very striking instances of disobedience by the children of Israel. The first was their refusal to drive out all the inhabitants of Canaan, as instructed by God. This refusal led to them and their children getting seduced into worshipping Baal, which angered God. The second instance of disobedience was after seeing the glory of Jehovah. They made and worshipped a golden calf when Moses climbed up Mount Sinai (Exodus 32).

Serve God with total submission

Our fear of God makes us submit to Him and one another in service. You see, when you are before a king, you ought to show decorum. This kind of behaviour would also be displayed in how you treat ordinary people. Therefore, in our service to God, submission is necessary. It demands that we be polite and show respect to everyone, especially elders (1 Peter 5:5).

When offering service, we ought to let other people have their way whenever possible and be selfless in all interactions (Philippians 2:3). When there is such submission, it is safe to say that God is honoured among the people. It reduces disagreements and drives away rancour. If it is a church where we serve, It will show humility and understanding, especially among the members.

Also, submission is so pertinent in Christianity that believers are required to submit to their leaders. They are to submit themselves to those in civil authority, even in the most challenging circumstances. (Genesis 16:9).

Serve God by divine direction

Honouring and seeking the will of God should be our goal in all of our services to Him. It should be placed beyond any form of gratification, even if we must lose. As strange as it may sound, we still need to know God's will even while trying to serve Him.

Happiness in the service of God can only be experienced when we know and do the will of the Lord. Anyone who knows God's big plan can begin to align with it, instead of acting like someone groping in the dark.

I have wondered about many things. For instance, would the life of Uzzah in the Bible have been saved if he had recourse to the instruction of God? Priests had instructions from the Lord concerning the Ark of the Covenant. It included how it was to be moved before putting it in a cart and trying to transport it at King David's behest (2 Samuel 6:1-7).

So, instead of getting emotional and wondering if the punishment given to Uzzah was fair, I try to remember the instructions given by God on how the Levites should move holy items. (Exodus 25:14-15).

That further strengthens the need to always seek God's will and direction on how to serve Him. First of all, are you called to serve? If the answer is yes, then my suggestion has always been to first of all find out how God wants you to go about it- if He hasn't already told you. Then do it exactly as He instructs.

Serve God with thanksgiving

Thanksgiving has a magnetic effect. It can draw more of whatever we are thankful for, to us. The psalmist wrote about his demeanour when approaching the house of God, knowing the power that is released when we thank and praise Him (Psalm 100:4).

Many people may look at their situations and wonder if there are good reasons to be thankful. Gloom may characterise our every gaze because of the problems of this world, but an atmosphere of joy is most conducive to attracting and keeping a move of God and His spirit.

Our thanksgiving is a way of acknowledging that the Lord is God, the one who made us and rewards us. Those who eventually get to know God always acknowledge that He is good and merciful.

Serve God with honesty

I grew up to learn that what I sow; is what I reap. It is always pertinent to make up our minds about our decision to serve God. We ought to serve with enthusiasm and do whatever is given to us to do with all our hearts. We must realise that God is right there watching and that He is the one who rewards us.

We must also display the virtue of honesty through all our dealings and words. God, as said earlier, is right there to bless us for our service, but we must be honest with ourselves first, then others too. Deception and pretence must be far from our service.

Serve God with reverence

Serving God acceptably, has an overall objective of pleasing Him. We have a responsibility to serve God with reverence and total obedience (Deuteronomy 13:4). That responsibility was spoken about in the book of Ecclesiastes (Ecclesiastes 12:13). To know what pleases God, review His word and instructions. Our emotions and wisdom will not do us any good.

Still, in the story of Uzzah, the man struck dead while trying to prevent the Ark of Covenant from falling. He died trying to transport it from his father's house to Jerusalem. What always strikes a chord for me and as it relates to service, is the importance of reverence for the things of God and His word. He lost his life because he touched the Ark irreverently. The lesson in this story for those of us who are in service is that reverence for God is critical.

Commenting on reverence, a much-respected teacher and prophet, Apostle Imeh Akpan, once spoke to us about how Obed of Edom stayed alive with the Ark of Covenant in his possession.

He explained that Obed's life was spared because he honoured the box and kept it safe. Within the three months that he had it in his possession, he used sticks to make boundaries around it which he never broke and would, from time to time, clean around these boundaries. God saw this and was pleased enough to bless him and his family.

Serve God in holiness

God does not just expect us to discover His will but to do it in holiness. Sin does not allow us to attain the purpose of God concerning our lives. In the Bible, Balaam, the prophet, knew this so well. That was why he was able to advise the Midianites on how to weaken the children of Israel. The plan was simple, weaken them by causing them to sin. So, at Peor, children of Israel were lured into sexual immorality with Midianite women (Numbers 31:14-16). As soon as this happened and they had gotten entangled in sin, the children of Israel became unholy. In that state, the children of Israel became vulnerable to sickness and disease. A plague came upon them and claimed the lives of many of them.

The world constantly finds ways to feed us with unholy materials to corrupt our thoughts and actions and cause us to be defeated by the devil. So, we must make a conscious effort to diligently guard our thoughts, to ensure that we remain holy in obedience to the will of God (1 Peter 1:15-16).

Serve God with the best

God is awesome. He deserves nothing but the best in the quality of whatever we render to Him, and this, I have always felt, includes the quality of offering, service and servants, among others.

Concerning gifts and offerings, there was a time when children of God gave sick and blind animals. So, to make them understand that He ought to have the best, God drew an analogy to gifts given to our earthly governors. Can we, His children, give sick and blind animals as gifts to our earthly leaders? Then why do we give Him less than the best? That does not require an answer but a lot of rumination and change in our attitudes to giving (Malachi 1:8).

As far as the quality of servants to serve is concerned, the Bible tells us how King Nebuchadnezzar of Babylon had his officials trained for three years to attain the level of skill and wisdom necessary for assignments in his palace (Daniel 1:3-5).

Now, if we train people for that long, would it not improve the quality of their service? We must realise the importance of deepening our training for ministers, even while on the job. They should also have opportunities to be the best they can be for the service they would perform.

Serve God in spirit and truth

Every true believer must serve God in spirit and truth. When we do that, our service becomes selfless, led by the Holy Spirit and aimed at pleasing God. It also displays love, endurance, goodness, meekness, faithfulness, joy, peace, kindness and self-control.

Jesus is also known as the word. This word was transformed into human form and even came to live among men. One of the words used by Jesus to describe Himself is "Truth". To serve God in truth is to be inspired and led by the word of God; it is to let Christ Jesus lead us.

Serve God with faithfulness

The children of Israel displayed a lack of faithfulness to the Almighty God, who brought them out of bitter slavery. They were quick to forget, grumble, complain and return to idolatry, which angered Him.

I have wondered how rewarding I would feel if I heard God say to me: "Well done, good and faithful servant!" To be faithful is to be loyal, true, trustworthy, dependable, and accurate. For our service to be acceptable, we must serve in faithfulness.

God wants us to care for and multiply what He puts in our hands. Church leaders at all levels are required to be faithful. They must look after the Lord's flock, tending to them and ensuring they are protected, multiplied, fed and guided (1 Corinthians 4:2).

We must look for the potential for faithfulness in individuals before considering them for appointment as stewards. The reward for faithful service is greater responsibility, and what a great honour to share in the Master's happiness (Mathew 25:23).

Serve God with gladness

Serving God with gladness pleases Him and enables us to enjoy peace. It preserves our victory and allows a move of the spirit of God. That is because we are supposed to serve the Lord with gladness (Psalm 100:2).

When the children of Israel forgot how good God had been to them and did not serve Him with joyfulness and gladness in their hearts, they paid for their actions because they knew no peace afterwards. They were given to their enemies to be yoked with iron and serve them in hunger, thirst, nakedness, and want of all things (Deuteronomy 28:47-48).

Gladness is not easy to hide. King David is described as someone who modelled what serving the Lord with gladness should be. He danced until his garment fell. He put aside the prevailing circumstance and just focused on the faithfulness and mercy of God.

Serve with diligence

I got to realise that service was an opportunity after reading Ecclesiastes 9:10. Anyone who understands the power in service stands to gain in many ways. Service is obedience. It causes the release of delayed blessings. It also leads to miraculous experiences. Diligence in the service of God involves faith, patience, carefulness and persistence.

There are rewards for those who serve God diligently, and we can be sure that our God, who is just, will release them (Hebrews 6:10-12). When diligent men are assigned to do the work of God, what will be received about them are good reports because there will always be progress (Ezra 5:8).

Leaders must always model diligence and allow God's spirit to guide them whenever they need to select people to assign tasks. In my life, I have seen men who served God all their lives and were even greatly influenced by one. I decided to imitate his attitude to service with a strong hope of the same reward. The Bible says that those who are diligent will surely experience:

- Wealth (Proverbs 10:4)

- Honour (Proverbs 22:2)

The Lord spoke to me one day in 2014. He talked about His service and made me know that in it were all the things that I was looking for at the time (money, work, family). Eventually, I understood how true this was and especially for those who serve with commitment (1 Corinthians 15:58).

Minimum supervision is a distinctive signature of diligent service. Diligent people are self-motivated and hardly ever need reminders concerning tasks they are assigned to perform. This group of people are dependable and can be trusted to execute sensitive tasks.

Diligence can be observed in the daily lifestyle of ants. Carefully watching them would reveal that they have no commander or overseer, yet they remain committed to gathering food as a daily task. (Proverbs 6:6-8).

Serve with humility

There is nothing we have that we were not given, including the opportunity to reach out to the lost. To be a minister is to become a servant of God, serving Him and others without any form of pride but with the full realisation that our call is nothing short of a privilege.

It is an error to think that without us, the work of God will not continue, but we must continually submit to one another because of our fear of He that called us (Ephesians 5:21).

Our Bishop once told us a story about how prophets in one of the previous churches he served went on something like a strike and refused to prophesy. They had grievances and wanted to send a message to the church elders. Then in one of the church meetings, by the power of the Holy Spirit, six new speaking prophets were revealed, and the work of God continued. Can you imagine that?

The word of God makes us appreciate how much God hates pride and resists those who are proud. Jesus models humility and asks that we learn of Him and ensure that we display the same humility He modelled (Mathew 11:29).

Serve God with a willingness

Many of us were appointed into ministerial offices before we even were formed in our mother's wombs. That means that the will of God concerning us would have already been in existence before we were even born. What God does in such instances is allow His plan for such people to be known to them. He expects them to accept and work towards achieving this plan willingly.

David, the man after God's heart, wrote about how he was delighted to do the will of God (Psalm 40:8). That was a sign of total obedience and submission, and only people with willing hearts can sincerely declare their delight to serve God as he did.

I have witnessed a man refuse the call of God to service. Whatever his reasons were, I cannot say, but I know that he was eventually required to pass the mantle to his son when he got home. I cannot remember seeing that brother after then and so can't say how things turned out. But the Bible tells us how things turned out for David, who accepted and did the will of God. He became a man enthroned, victorious and honoured.

Serve with expectation

Service is an act of worship and comes with its rewards. The woman with the issue of blood, who had been bleeding for twelve years, had an expectation. The Bible records that she said to herself, "If only I can touch the hem of His garment, I will be healed" (Mark 5:25-29).

As we delight ourselves in the service of the Lord, we should expect that He will keep His word concerning those that serve Him to give them the desires of their hearts (Psalm 37:4)

Therefore we ought to bring into our service an attitude of earnest expectation from the perspective of faith. Such an attitude also pleases the Lord (Hebrews 11:6), and we can keep doing His work with the knowledge that the expectation of a righteous person can never be cut off (Proverbs 23:18).

RESOURCES NEEDED TO SERVE GOD

The first step we should take as people who wish to serve God is to make ourselves available. It all starts with a made-up mind to be there for God. Nobody can decide to serve God for another because it requires a lot of sacrifice in money, time and skill.

A person going into service must be a giver-someone concerned about others and values them even above self. The desire to show off or exert control over others must never motivate service because it promotes self, while all service to God must be for the benefit of others (Philippians 2:3-5).

Also, the strength needed to serve comes from God Himself. If we, in any way, depend on another source for it, then we cannot glorify Him and easily get burnt out and frustrated while working for Him.

That is probably one of the most common reasons why we see some folks burning hot for the Lord this moment and the next, so worn out that everyone can see a clear display of apathy towards the things of God (1 Peter 4:11).

Our Time

Serving God requires that we invest a lot of time. Sometimes, cutting out a lot of profitless endeavours from our lives helps achieve this. The Lord told me one day that as I was doing His work, He would be doing mine too. That meant that the times I spent cleaning the seats in the church for Him, He, in return, was cleaning my life, and when I sang for Him, He was clearing the obstacles in my life.

It is such a powerful principle that those who give God their time; receive corresponding care from Him. That is why Most Reverend N.D Ayakndue, during the commissioning of a worship centre in Abuja, was bold enough to say: "The Lord never uses and dumps". He rewards us for the time we spend serving Him.

Our skill

We all have one skill or the other that we can use in the service of God. He has given us varying skills, wisdom and knowledge to drive the work of His kingdom.

The Bible contains a story about how in the time of Moses, the people built a sanctuary for God. For the project to start, people had to give. Some gave in kind, while others, who were skilled, willingly offered their services. Moses had to mobilise skilled workers, and the book of Exodus says:

"So Bezalel, Oholiab and every skilled person to whom the LORD has given skill and ability to know how to carry out all the work of constructing the sanctuary are to do the work just as the LORD has commanded."

Then Moses summoned Bezalel and Oholiab and every skilled person to whom the LORD had given ability and who was willing to come and do the work" (Exodus 36:1-2).

One time when I had no money to contribute to a planned church activity, I offered to drive. That was the least I felt I could do. I had an old and spacious Volvo that was very useful in moving people and equipment here and there. It turned out that my contribution, through my vehicle, was also valuable to the success of that activity.

I am sure there were times when it seemed we had nothing to contribute. But I am saying that because the resources we need are tangible and intangible, there is always something to contribute.

The story I just told makes it clear that there is always something that God has given to us in the form of skill and wisdom that can be used for His glory. Some blessings are attached to giving while in the service of God, and as much as possible, we must aim to partake.

Our intellect

Have you ever wondered how many of the tools used in our churches get put together? I am talking about the manuals, yearly planners, music and others like them. People take the time to put all these resources together by applying their creativity continuously.

We can all contribute our intellect in one way or the other. I have heard of people who have written Sunday School Manuals for decades, and boy! That is such a big motivation for the rest of us, isn't it?

Our strength

That is one resource that can never be too much, whether individually or collectively, physically or spiritually. Joyfully executing whatever task assigned to us in God's vineyard is the strength that keeps us going until we receive our miracle.

After completing my secondary education, I did a lot of work in my local church while waiting to gain admission into the university. I did whatever I could find to do and joyfully joined in the dirtiest, roughest and toughest tasks in the church. So one day, after a tiring church compound weeding, I hurriedly rushed back home tired and hungry.

When I got there, I met everyone in really high spirits and my mother, particularly, cheered me repeatedly and excitedly. I stood looking at them and asked them to quit the drama and "Please" Tell me what had happened. Then my mother, who was holding an envelope addressed to me in my handwriting, immediately handed it over to me, smiling. As I quickly removed its content and started reading, I discovered that it was my admission letter to one of the federal universities. That was my reward.

Our prayers

Every ministry needs to be immersed in prayer to succeed. Prayer is one key that opens the door to success in the work of God.

Many churches discover its importance and establish prayer groups saddled with the responsibility of seeking the face of the Lord concerning all matters and which usually meet before key church activities.

Prayer releases the power needed to drive the work of God. This power is the force behind the move of the Holy Spirit at services, vigils and crusades. Prayer is a resource needed for success. It enables the power of God to be released, for the benefit of His children. We must pray to activate this power. We must turn the house of God into a one of prayer by volunteering to seek His face each time we meet (Isaiah 56:7).

Our finance

There is always something to do in the house of God. That does not mean we should contend for service areas or positions with others but instead look for uncovered service areas to fill.

These days, money can be helpful to the work of the kingdom. We are talking about tithes, offerings, seeds, donations etc. Giving is pertinent in executing kingdom projects.

Money is a helpful resource in the service of God. When there is a need and corresponding call to give, it is an opportunity to be blessed and the wise, who are always willing to take a leap of faith, always respond.

In the time of Moses, people had what we may describe as: "The giver's attitude". They gave until what they gathered exceeded what was required

(Exodus 36:5).

When my church was under construction, I decided in my heart, to be part of it, and looked for areas I could contribute. After I made this decision, the Lord, who heard me that day and supplies everything, made provision for me to give and be blessed. A couple of months later, I discovered that while I was building His house, He was building mine too.

THE BENEFITS OF SERVING GOD

When we serve God, we qualify for certain rewards. The psalmist felt the need to bless the Lord and bring to our attention how He gives us multiple benefits, which come daily (Psalm 68:19).

God, who is not unjust, will not forget the service we render to Him with love and reverence. What He would do instead is, reward us according to our expectations (Hebrews 6:10).

The book of Exodus contains two scriptures that can help us articulate some of the benefits of serving God. When we read them, we will be able to highlight, very succinctly, the benefits that they point to.

The first scripture records God talking to his people, the Israelites, with a promise, if they would serve Him. He said to them:

"You shall serve the Lord your God, and He will bless your bread and your water, and I will take sickness away from among you. None shall miscarry or be barren in your land; I will fulfil the number of your days" (Exodus 23:25-26 ESV).

The second scripture was God sending Moses to the King of Egypt, instructing him to free the Hebrews. The reason given by Him for their freedom was service. They were to be released to go and serve God. The point here is, those who serve God must be free to do so and to Him alone. Therefore, we can say that serving God has the power to free us from evil captivity. To begin the process of setting the Hebrews free, God gave this instruction:

"And the LORD said unto Moses, Rise early in the morning, and stand before Pharaoh, and say unto him, Thus saith the LORD God of the Hebrews, Let my people go, that they may serve me" (Exodus 9:13 KJV).

From the two scriptures mentioned above, it is clear what serving God can do for us. There are benefits we can look forward to with excitement and hope. I know there might be more, so please feel free to add to the list. For now, we are sure that serving God would lead to the following five pertinent and powerful things in our lives:

1. God will provide for us plentifully and prevent what we eat or drink from causing any harm to us.

2. He will keep us healthy.

3. He will ensure that we are fruitful in our bodies and all we do. Yokes and covenants attached to barrenness and delays in having children will

break.

4. We will live long lives.

5. We will be set free from bondage, slavery and oppression.

CHAPTER 6
Spreading the Good News

"Preach the gospel at all times and when necessary, use words"
- *St Francis of Assisi*

Young Christians sometimes find the charge to reach out to the world with the message of salvation a big challenge. Much like I did, many shy away from this responsibility or generally find it unnecessary. Many of them have also described it as being "Terribly inconvenient".

Nobody said that it would be easy or convenient. It is, however, necessary. Besides, God never said that we would have no inconvenience or that walking with Him would be easy. God has assured us of his guidance, protection and power as we go out.

Spreading the Good News is a command and a responsibility. When we get saved, we are saddled with the responsibility to help others get saved and ought to respond in obedience. Jesus commands us to go into the world and preach the Good News to all creation (Mark 16:15). He also tells us who, how and what to say as part of the task.

Remember, one of the ways to show our wisdom and prove our obedience to the will of God is soul-winning. The book of wisdom (Proverbs 11:30) tells us that when we get saved, we become a tree of life, and when we help others get saved, we are wise.

Like many others, I had always found going out to win souls difficult and sometimes even a bit embarrassing. It was hard for me to take my Bible and speak to strangers about Jesus, and I know that some of you reading this can relate to what I am saying.

A critical look back at my life in retrospect revealed the reason for my apathy in spreading the Good News. In all honesty, because I had not completely dealt with my sins, I could not get myself to embrace and respond to the salvation I had found appropriately. I had no motivation to share my faith and testimony with others.

It certainly helps to speak to others about Jesus from an informed angle. When you know the Lord, talking about him becomes easy; the words flow out of you naturally. That is perhaps why the Bible encourages us to study to show ourselves approved so that without shame, we can correctly speak about Jesus to others (2 Timothy 2:15).

One day, after teaching, my pastor was asked what the question was since he was fond of saying that Jesus was the answer. Such questions can only be answered by those who study the word and understand why Jesus came.

Many churches pay lip service to evangelism, thereby raising young Christians who shy away from going out to get others saved. The truth is that if we value our salvation, we should stop at nothing in telling the whole world about this it. The church should drive efforts to help individuals deal with the issue of how to break the hold of sinfulness so that they can find deliverance to enjoy the full benefits of their salvation.

All leaders in the church must show themselves as worthy examples, and in like manner, we are also supposed to go out and be examples to the world. That is one power-filled way to get the attention of people around us concerning the Good News we carry. Christ Jesus should be the answer to the question asked by the world concerning who God is. He is the only way to be reconciled to Him.

WHAT EXACTLY IS THIS GOOD NEWS?

In Nigeria, when laws and schemes created by the government are supposed to be in the best interest of citizens, it usually takes a lot of awareness creation by individuals and Non-Governmental Organisations to get the populace to understand and in many instances, derive any form of benefit.

The reason for that trend is usually because these individuals and organisations either took part in advocating for these laws and schemes or have taken time to study to unbundle them to the public. They invest all this time and effort because they believe that the change to come would be in the best interest of all.

Similarly, right from the time of the early church at Antioch, having first received the Good News and partaken in the divine salvation it brings, it became not just a thing of obedience to spread the news and get others saved but also a decent thing. They go out and tell others about it.

Our Lord Jesus, while here with us, proclaimed this Good News and commanded all His disciples to tell as many people, in as many places as they could, about it. The goal was to get them to repent for their sins and reconcile with God through the Good News.

So what is this Good News our Lord wants us to tell everyone? What exactly changed that required wide publicity? I mean, how were things before the coming of the so-called "Good News"? My pastor liked to refer to whatever it was as the "Bad News". And I would like to use his term to explain the old situation of man and his broken relationship with God, as compared to the new opportunity now available to him to re-establish or strengthen it.

Bad News	**Good News**
Sin	Repentance
Loss of glory	Reconciliation
God's wrath/condemnation	Deliverance

God's thoughts are always with us because He loves and cares for us deeply. One Bible passage I love so much tells of how He has crowned man with glory and honour, after which He put him in charge of all creation. (Psalm 8:4-8)

We were all created by God to dominate our world and by a divine mandate. God created us to be like him, both in appearance and character. It is this God-like nature that we possess, that ensures that we remain in glory.

A close examination of the story of the children of Israel reveals how the Lord had delivered them from slavery. That was after they remembered Him and cried out to Him in distress. They were stubborn people and would always find a reason to stray back into sinful lives, which always incurred God's wrath.

God promised the Israelites good health, prosperity, victory and more if they would remain true to Him. But they weren't and now and then, found themselves again and again in bitter captivity.

Small wonder because those who play with sin face the likelihood of sickness, failure and eventual captivity. It became clearer why I had suffered so many setbacks personally- I never truly repented and received the Good News. Though I was aware of it, I had never really reached the point of total surrender. (Mark 1:15).

Since the beginning of the world, sin has been man's treacherous enemy, responsible for the consistent loss of his crown of glory and honour, given to him by God and thereby exposing him to disgrace and shame. Many people cannot exert healthy dominance in life like God intended when He created us. The ability to do this comes through living in righteousness. (Proverbs 14:34). Sin also placed people in positions of enmity with God and stirred up God's righteous anger, which was the "Bad news".

The Good News grows from the love that God has for us and His unwillingness to allow us to perish. We were unable to live by the law given by Him in Bible times, so because of His love for us, He found us a ransom that would liberate us once and for all from our sins and resultant estrangement from Him. That's the Good News referred to in the gospel that Jesus proclaimed and came to fulfil (Mark 10:45).

The Good News can also be described as the gospel of reconciliation- a message proclaimed by Christ Jesus Himself, which calls us to timely repentance from our sins and saves us from the righteous wrath of God.

To repent does not end in confessions but in staying away from whatever sinful acts were previously committed. I mean running away and staying there. If you are living a life of fornication, you must quickly stop. If you live in the same house with a partner you are married to, that is sinful. Do not waste any time. Move out. Do not be afraid.

Making such a change may cause you a slight difficulty, but all that will eventually pass, and you will be truly free. Also, learning to commit every decision to God, especially life-changing ones like choosing a life partner, as advised, must start with a fast, then fervent prayer and even prophetic enquiry. That, in my opinion, will reduce the likelihood of experiencing the pains that a wrong choice can bring.

Like in my case, the Good News will mean nothing much to you until you begin to tap into its transformative power.

When we become aware of the price that Jesus paid for our freedom and restoration, our prayer to accept Him as Lord and Saviour and our baptism begin to make sense to us. We can then take up our sonship with understanding- which helps us turn our backs on the things of the world in the total renewal of minds.

That process can be described as freedom from our past and empowerment for our future. It happens through faith in the redemptive sacrifice of Jesus. After experiencing all of these, we are better prepared to go out and get others saved to fulfil the ministry committed to us by our Lord (2 Corinthians 5:17-19).

BENEFITS OF SOUL-WINNING

There can be no soul-winning until we accept the ministry of reconciliation committed to us in the second book of Corinthians. It's such a transformative principle that brings with it copious blessings. I believe our lives can either draw people to God or push them away from Him.

Many people do not just live sinful lives but are reasons why others fall into it. We must all be careful not to cause those with weak consciences who are not so mature at heart to fall into sin. God prefers that such persons have millstones hung around their necks and thrown into the sea. Such a stand by God conveys to us the magnitude of His displeasure in such an influence (1 Corinthians 8:12).

The first thing about us that wins souls is indeed our character. As Christians, especially leaders, the Lord wants us to always show an example to those around us through our lifestyles. Our words and actions should promote love, peace and the immeasurable power of God. I weep in my heart when I read news of pastors falling below society's moral pass mark. There is no need to articulate why we have so many damaging stories about Christian leaders. That is a discussion for another day.

However, if we feel the process of choosing our leaders is flawed or the characters mentioned or plots in the stories we hear and read are distorted or fake. The word of God can transform men and women across the world, even the vilest of them.

We must not lord what we stand for over others but must be models to the flock if we intend to retain our crowns of glory and honour (1 Peter 5:3-4). That is where soul-winning starts.

What we wear, where we go, the friends we keep, the music we listen to, the movies we watch, the way we treat our spouse, our conduct in the office, our lifestyle after Sunday Service and the list goes on and on, must be examples also approved by God.

Many years ago, I met this handsome and at the time, interesting young man during a visit to one of the African countries. We immediately became friends. He had been working in that country as a night-time Disc Jockey while I was just passing through town.

On one occasion, we stood together by a café with cigarettes in hand and enjoying each other's company when one woman from one of the buses that had just parked nearby briskly walked straight to us. She asked if we were Christians and why we were wasting our time and good looks instead of using them to serve the Lord Jesus.

The question and comments made by this woman softened me at first. Then I surveyed the composure of my defiant friend, who seemed untouched by anyway and became emboldened. Seeing this, she continued, trying her best to reach out to us until we were eventually saved from her persistence by the sound of the horn of her bus. The blare of the horn signalled to its passengers that it was time to continue their journey. It rescued us from her by forcing her to hurry away. I won't forget her many questions, almost to the point of tears. She made me examine my life afterwards.

I eventually broke all communication with my friend. As I write, I hope God has touched him just as He touched me. I am also glad that I had such experiences in my life to share with others. As for that woman, I am happy she obeyed God and spoke to us that day. Whoever she was, I sincerely wish she could see me now. I know she would bless the Lord for my transformation. I hope that writing this story will encourage someone to change too. It is a story of the transformative power of soul-winning. It is also about a woman bold enough to obey God and speak to two young men. I will always appreciate what she did. There are several benefits of reaching out to people.

It releases the power of the Holy Ghost

When we model or speak to people about Christ, it is always incredible to see how the spirit of God convicts them and causes them to repent. I know people who heard the gospel and changed their professions, and I also know a few that changed where they lived just to be able to serve God.

A pastor once told me a story of evangelists who went to preach in a hostile territory where preachers were not welcome. They gathered a crowd close to the market and started speaking to them about Christ Jesus.

While they were at it, a group of armed and angry men suddenly showed up and asked who gave the evangelists the right to preach in their town. The preachers were forced, by the arrival of the men, to stop what they were doing.

Within minutes, the leader of the men passed a quick judgment for the offence committed, requiring the heads of the preachers. On hearing this, many of the preachers trembled with fear, but one became bold and spoke to the lead assailant. He stressed that they had done no wrong but gather people who were poor, blind and lame. He also asked if they would be released if the blind saw again.

The leader laughed at the request before him; the evangelist began to pray and ask God for a revelation of his power. His colleagues were still trembling, with their faces filled with dismay, when shouts started coming from within the crowd. One person here, then another there, and another, until they were coming from almost everywhere. Those were the shouts of people who started getting healed. Blind people began to see, and the lame stood to their feet.

In no time, the shouts had become jubilation. There was excitement as much as there was dust in the air. You can imagine what the Holy Spirit did that day. Well, as the story goes, the assailants spared the lives of the preachers after witnessing those miracles. It did not stop there, as the evangelists were even escorted safely out of town.

It gives divine health

There is always a difference between those who serve God and those who do not. Soul winning is service to God and comes with rewards. When we serve God, He blesses whatever we eat and drink and takes away sicknesses. He does not allow those that serve Him to miscarry or stay barren. They experience long lives because He stops whatever may lead to premature death (Exodus 23:25-26).

All that is required of us to experience the promise above is to obey God in everything. Like true ambassadors of Christ, as we do this, we become a source of health to even the people we reach out to, thereby sharing with them what we have received while also enjoying ourselves as we do so (Proverbs 13:17 KJV).

Our hands become clean

When we have the opportunity to save the lost and fail to do so, we risk our hands being stained with their blood if they perish. The truth is that we will account for all our actions and words in this life. That includes our neglect of opportunities to save the lost.

I know that there are modern-day Jonahs, who, when the Lord gives them a message as prophets, end up refusing to deliver it. Others with the gift of healing may also refuse to exercise it. There is no real difference between these people; they are all in the same category and will certainly give an account of their actions.

The Lord expects that when He sends a message to someone with whom He is displeased, His servants will ensure that they warn such a person and try to get that person to repent. If they have a chance to do this but fail to, then the blood of that fellow will become a stain on their hands, but if they succeed in warning the person, their hands become clean (Ezekiel 3:18).

We must passionately view "The lost" As our responsibility and help them find their way back to the Lord in reconciliation, just as we were. A good number of those who need our help are depressed, battered and bruised. We must help attend to every form of spiritual starvation that they face.

Since we, these days, witness a fakeness of outward appearances, it may be shocking to know that many of those we call "The lost" Are in our churches. Therefore, we must make haste to ensure that the purpose and power of the Good News touch them to save and transform them. We should also pray that they find strength in the joy of the Lord.

CHAPTER 7
Belaying Profanity

"May I govern my passions with absolute sway, and grow wiser and better as life wears away"
-        *Isaac Watts*

They say, "Information is power" However, the freedom that comes from "Knowing" These days can be easy to abuse. Such abuse is especially so when lines are crossed, like the one that separates freedom from profanity.

Social Media is awash with many types of profanities displayed by many reckless young people without recourse to possible consequences. No opportunity is lost where the show of utter disrespect is concerned in many social media communications. Recently, very prominent men of God have been victims of these profanities. Please believe me when I say that this could well be a trap.

A profane man does not give spiritual things the seriousness that they deserve. He is more likely to treat them with levity. God will not commit anything of spiritual value into the hand of such a person, who will likely treat it with disdain, or in a way that will not show that it has any value.

Profanity can stop a young man from getting the best from God and can even expose him to curses and future pain. Many young people are oblivious to the superiority of spiritual things over natural ones, and so fail to harness its benefits. In life, special effort must be made, including erring on the side of caution, if necessary, when it comes to appreciating the value of spiritual things- to avoid falling into profanity through our actions or speech.

The profane do not consider the spiritual implication of their actions and speech and show the least degree of accountability. Our actions can bring God's judgement upon us, something that we must avoid at all costs (Ezekiel 24:14).

A popularly used adage says that: "Actions speak louder than words". Small wonder we are warned that all actions will be judged on the last day (Ecclesiastes 12:14). As for our speech, it is pertinent to realise that they act as pointers to the quality of our character. We must ensure that we avoid behaving or speaking profanely because our words, like our actions, will be judged (Mathew 12:36-37).

In the Bible, there are accounts of people whose actions and words produced certain results that can help us in this current time to appreciate the spiritual power that accompanies our actions and speech. To show how powerful our actions and words can be, it is important to point out that when we speak, heaven releases power to bring what we say to manifestation. So, being mindful of this can be very helpful in keeping us away from profanity. We shall examine some Bible accounts to make that clearer.

PROFANITY THROUGH SPEECH

Profanity stops us from getting the best from God at any particular point in time. One of the earliest profane people, as recorded in the Bible, was Esau. He did not place value on his birthright, so when his brother demanded that he speaks words to relinquish it, he thought they were mere words or ordinary talk and agreed. The Bible even recorded that he asked what use the birthright was to him if he starved to death (Genesis 25).

Many people act this same way even today. They become careless and fail to acknowledge that the tongue carries great power. It can release words that can build and those that can destroy.

Also, when a patriarch releases blessings, heaven backs them up to the detriment of profane people. Therefore, by the time Esau realised what had happened to him, it was too late, his father had already pronounced the blessings on his brother- Jacob (Hebrews 12:16-17). Imagine if the reverse were the case, we would probably call God: "The God of Abraham, Isaac and Esau", Today.

PROFANITY THROUGH ACTION

The message is that God cannot transmit anything of spiritual significance to profane people. Let us review another account of profanity in the Bible, right in the house of Jacob and his twelve sons. He cursed his first son, Rueben, for dishonouring him by having an intimate relationship with his concubine. Such dishonour was not to be without consequences (Genesis 49:2-4).

Rueben was so profane that he did not take the words of Jacob, his father, seriously. His unseriousness was evident in his failure to plead for a change of the verdict. He did not attempt to pacify his father.

Jacob, who was the patriarch of the family, was near his death and had gathered his children to bless them. But rather than bless his firstborn- Reuben, Jacob cursed him.

Reuben's reaction or lack of an appropriate one proved his heart was full of profanity. It showed when he, knowing the significance of his father's last words, did not bother to cry out or plead to make him change his mind or reverse them. Instead, he chose to take the words of his father lightly, which is typical of a profane person.

Today, profanity has robbed many persons of God's blessings and brought suffering to just as many. The consequences of profane actions are noticeable in the lives of innocent children. Down the line, as was the case of the tribe of Rueben, his children suffered because of his profanity. That lasted for five hundred years until Moses was about to die and prayed to God to turn their situation around (Deuteronomy 33:6).

The absence of regard for spiritual things can be observed in the church at moments when blessings are pronounced, prayers offered or worship made. It is common to see careless people engage in other activities and put no value on these spiritual exercises.

Many of them, during prayer and worship sessions, can be observed to be disconnected, with their attentions drawn to salutations and discussions with friends. I once observed a lady in a supposed holy action, while the pastor was praying for the congregation, telling a couple who were attending church for the first time not to sit together. I could see from the face of the man she was talking to that he was distracted and confused. The man and his wife were trying to connect to what was going on at the altar, but this lady was busy trying to let them know that men sit at the extreme right and women, on the left.

Truly, many prefer to be preoccupied with letting first-timers know that in church, women dress in a certain way or that families sit this or that way. I think that this is fine but may not be necessary at first.

Newcomers to church eventually and easily adjust if they are encouraged to develop a sense of belonging. While this is going on, be sure that the Holy Spirit remains at work on them. We should also model our good virtues for newcomers to imbibe, if we do that, we may not need to speak so much to them. What happens is that they will observe and copy us.

Sometimes even church leaders act as though the same spiritual principles that apply to members do not apply to them. That is also profanity. They are slow to participate in praises and even find it hard to flip the pages of their Bibles as verses get mentioned. They, of course, miss blessing by doing so.

There is no immunity from spiritual things for a young pastor or church elder who does not heed spiritual instruction. Apart from the possibility that a blessing may be missed, such leaders also show a bad example to others. For example, the instructions about the principle of tithing are clear, leaders who do not obey them will, in the company of whoever follows their example, not enjoy the blessings that tithing brings.

The Lord spoke to us one day in a meeting. He talked about those of us who eat from His table and that of the devil. You might be wondering what that means. We are expected to have turned our backs on heathen practices and the worship and consultation of gods through mediums and witchcraft, but it still happens!

Certainly, you must have heard that Christians participate in cultural practices like celebrating and eating the so-called, "New Yam" or even swallowing charms for protection, after which they return to the church to partake in the "Lord's Table". That is very dangerous! Christians who participate in festivals that glorify the devil and seek solutions to their problems from satanic sources must avoid the Holy

Communion and immediately seek deliverance. God remains merciful; we must stop our profanity through these detestable acts.

CHAPTER 8
Those Especially Loved

"My son, hear the instruction of thy father, and forsake not the law of thy mother"
- King Solomon

God loves all of us. He promises never to leave or forsake us. However, some of us are especially loved. Getting into this category should be the aspiration of every young person who wants to enjoy special privileges.

King David, right from the time of his youth, enjoyed God's special privileges. He testified to His love and loyalty (Psalm 89:24 GNT). That was in addition to being described in the Bible as a man after God's heart.

Bishop E.U. Ekwere (Rear admiral Retired) once described loyalty as: "I do not always agree with you, but I will always support you". Can you appreciate the message in that statement? So, for God, who has been the standard for loyalty, to declare His love and loyalty to King David, it is wise to examine his character to find out what he did differently.

The description of King David as a man after God's heart came about through his character. God took notice of his character and the sincerity of his heart before declaring that he was after His heart. David assumed a special status that caused the Lord to release benefits to him.

GOD'S LOVE AND LOYALTY

There is no better-recorded example of God's love and loyalty to man than that found in the Davidic story. This story contains accounts of many benefits enjoyed by a King who started his life as a shepherd and ended up in a palace.

The favour of God preserved David and gave him victory over his enemies. It made God reckon with him and choose him to father the greatest king that lives (Jesus). Before we look into David's character, let us dig deep to get out the benefits of being especially loved by God.

We find God's favour

When we are especially loved by God, the first thing we enjoy is favour. The favour of God is the grace we require in our daily prayers. It is the supply of unmerited goodness and mercy. So, when we talk about the favour of God, it refers to the faithful actions of God in our lives.

When the children of Israel inherited vineyards that they did not plant, it was grace. When earthly fathers did good things for their sons that was grace also. Likewise, when we enjoy exceeding favour from our heavenly father, we are experiencing grace too. This assurance made David declare his confidence that he would enjoy the goodness and mercy of God for as long as he lived (Psalm 23:6).

Consistent victory

The Lord made David triumph over his enemies and those of Israel even as a young boy. The story of his defeat of the Philistine giant– Goliath, with a sling and a stone, assures us of victory despite the size of whatever challenge we face.

It also assures us of a solution if conventional options are absent. God can make us champions in the most challenging situations (1 Samuel 17:50 NIV).

We qualify for divine selection

Today, many leaders are selected because they can write fat cheques or look charismatic. But in having Samuel choose the least of Jesse's sons to be the King, God demonstrated that the way to choose a Godly leader, especially in the church, is to gain an insight into the heart of whoever is under consideration. He expects us to turn to Him, who alone can read the hearts of men.

When our hearts are committed to obeying God in all things, He chooses us and sends the Holy Spirit to help us in leadership (1 Samuel 16:7).

We find a need for forgiveness

People who boldly sin and shamelessly defend or try to cover them up do not end well. A person with a heart humble enough to accept wrong and seek true repentance always receives God's pardon because God is always delighted to show repentant sinners mercy. David acknowledged his sin and immediately repented, and the Lord forgave him (2 Samuel 12:12-13).

We find strength

In the most draining circumstances, the Lord released strength to David. While the people around him were bitter and in low spirits, David was given power by his God.

It was this strength and the ability to reflect on the promises of God that gave David the hope by which he encouraged himself at the difficult times of his life, which eventually strengthened him for the victory that was to come (1 Samuel 30:6 NIV).

We attract God's covenant

Whenever God visits a man, He makes a covenant with him as He did in the life of our Father Abraham.

The assurance that God keeps His covenants comes from how He has dealt with people from Bibble times (Ruth 2:20 GNT).

This passage from the book of Ruth in the Bible tells us about a promise made by God to David that one of his descendants would rule forever. The fulfilment of that promise was the coming of Jesus Christ (Romans 1:3).

We receive anointing

Since the day that Prophet Samuel anointed David as King, the Holy Spirit came upon him and began to prepare him for leadership. The spirit empowered him as he faced the many difficulties that confronted him in preparation for the throne of Israel (1 Samuel 16:13).

A LOOK INTO KING DAVID'S CHARACTER

A close examination of the character of King David will further help us understand why he pleased God so much as to attract His love and loyalty.

If we possess the kind of heart that the shepherd boy- turned King of Israel had, we will surely get the attention of God and hopefully win His special love.

In a blog by Ron Edmondson, ten character traits of King David from the Bible's account of his life were reviewed. I will share these character traits, including one more that I feel is necessary to add.

David had humility

Our society promotes pride and arrogance. God is not pleased with proud people. Right from the times of our fathers, God used humble people.

Moses was humbled after he escaped from Egypt. The Bible described him as the meekest man, and his ministry did not start until many years later after he had learned humility in the desert as a shepherd (Numbers 12:3 NIV). He was 80 years old when he first appeared before Ramses, Pharaoh of Egypt.

One powerful character trait of David was his humility. He was humble enough to have acknowledged the Lord's anointed- Saul and would not hurt him, even when the opportunity was right before him, especially considering the ill intentions displayed earlier by Saul.

David expressed the opinion that all humans, whether great or small, were like a puff of breath. We all eventually disappear. This view meant that being proud was foolish and pointless because we had no control over our lives (Psalm 62:9).

David had reverence

David had reverence for God. He always displayed a reverential fear for the Lord. That, in turn, guided him in wisdom. He also understood that his reverence for and obedience to the Lord in everything was the key to him and his descendants remaining on the throne. He even communicated this to his son- Solomon before he died.

King David's wife, Michal, on the other hand, despised her husband for dancing so much for the Lord that his robe fell. As punishment for doing this, she turned out to be the only woman recorded in the Bible to have ended up barren. David understood the role the Lord played in his destiny and so must we if we want to get His attention.

David was respectful

Social etiquette requires that we report the shortcomings of representatives of persons or companies to their principals. It is outright disrespect for an individual or institution to harm another's representative on active duty, especially if that representative was sent by the highest authority in the land (Romans 14:4).

The Lord instructs us not to touch His anointed ones and not to hurt His prophets (1chronicles 16:22). Church leaders fall into this category. They are God's anointed.

Since we are not omnipresent like God, we are likely to be ignorant of the oil on the heads of men of God and so are best advised to just avoid causing any form of harm to any of them or anyone who does God's work.

The harm referred to here can be physical or even online- a common practice today. Acting otherwise shows a lack of respect for God and is inconsistent with the character of David.

King David's deep respect for the Lord, was further reflected in his handling of Saul's jealousy and hostility. Twice he had the opportunity to harm King Saul but spared him. He refused to kill or allow any of his men to harm Saul, who had made no secret of his intention to kill him. Instead, he waved a cut piece of Saul's robe to indicate that he could have killed him but did not. He did this because Saul was his master and the Lord's anointed (1 Samuel 24:10).

David was trusting

Trust can best be described after watching children. Small wonder Jesus recommended that we be like them to enter the kingdom (Mathew 18:3). Daddy throws his child into the air, and the kid keeps smiling and shows no fear as if to let whoever is watching know that he trusts that Daddy won't let him fall. That is because where there is trust, fear is absent.

We all need to develop a trustful attitude towards our father in heaven. If someone were searching for the key to King David's fearless demeanour, a great place to start would be Psalm 27:1. The Lord was described as light, salvation and stronghold. The realisation of who God is drives away fear.

To develop trust, we must seek the light, salvation and strength that the Lord provides. To receive light, it is pertinent to start engaging with the word of God (Psalm 119:130).

Salvation comes from the power of the Holy Spirit that transforms our hearts. A stronghold is a defensive structure in times of trouble, which makes us inaccessible to our enemies. Even when David stayed in the desert and hill strongholds of Ziph (1 Samuel 23:14), he knew that the real power that kept him alive was the Lord.

To trust God today, we must, first of all, know Him. Through stories written in the Bible, we can study how He interacted with those before us to understand His character. We must earnestly seek him.

David was loving

David expressed his love for God in the first verse of the eighteenth Psalm. It is not hard to identify a man who loves his neighbours because He will be careful to live peacefully with them. He would ensure that none of his actions brings displeasure or hurt to them. That is similar to when a man loves God. He would ensure that he never displeases Him and takes time to do all that is expected of him.

David's love for God brought him favour, wealth, victory, divine strength, forgiveness and an everlasting covenant that his descendants would rule forever. The truth is that our God is always moved to do great things for those who love him. He is prepared to give such people the earth and even much more. No one can quantify or imagine in advance what He prepares for them (1 Corinthians 2:9).

David was devoted

In my church, as was common in many others, there was a committee responsible for following up with members and new converts to ensure that they settle in easily and grow spiritually. Members of this committee visit and call new members when necessary. Their work was usually to encourage and sometimes find out if there were challenges whenever members, especially new ones, were absent from service.

I used to be a member of this committee. One day during a visit by some committee members to a new church member- who had not been in church for a while, I heard the lady ask how she was expected to serve God without money. That was not the first time I had heard something like that, but what got me thinking was hearing that she further stressed that if God wanted her to serve Him, He would have to provide the finance and other blessings needed for her to do so.

She reminded me of what experience had taught me about how God makes a way where there seems to be none. I had once been so determined to be in the church that despite my broken down vehicle, empty pocket and the church being over five kilometres away, I was not discouraged. Instead, I planned an early trek, but guess what? I never did. God just never allowed it. He saw my devotion and made a way for me.

David wrote about how glad he was when he was invited to God's house, where he hoped to spend the rest of his life in fellowship with Him. David's loyalty to God was expressed in his claim to God as his God, the God of his salvation and his Lord. It was further expressed in the quality of his sacrifices, his energetic dance, the nature of his praise and his willingness to do whatever God wanted him to do. The satisfaction he derived from his love and devotion to God, was expressed in his Psalms (Psalm 4:7).

David recognised God

Have you acknowledged the powerful deeds of God in your life? King David did this (Psalm 9:1). He praised God for His wonderful works. The same king demonstrated his recognition of the special role played by the Lord in his life by declaring that he would not give God what costs him nothing (2 Samuel 24:24).

In addition to our love for God, we are expected to acknowledge Him in all we do (Proverbs 3:5-6). The necessity to do so is if we want Him to direct all that we do.

As a king, David knew the importance of having God direct his decisions- a privilege he enjoyed, evidenced by his countless victories over his enemies. The point here is that when we appreciate God and give Him the required recognition He deserves- as the captain of every aspect of our lives; we invite victory.

David was obedient

King David knew the importance of obeying God's instructions, and so even on his deathbed, he advised his son Solomon to do the same. He wrote about how he loved God's law and had hidden it in his heart to ensure he followed it and lived blameless before a God he knew was holy.

The Lord, on His part, spoke about King David's obedience. He described him as a man ready to obey Him in everything. Total obedience to God is a kingly attribute and of great importance to those who want God's attention and loyalty (Acts 13:22).

David was repentant

There was a time when sin was something to be ashamed of. The shame could even be noticed when a sinner confessed. Nowadays, many people seem so proud of their lives of sin. They become proud liars, fornicators and murderers. People who try to cover their sins always end up with more. Most liars need even bigger lies to stay covered up.

King David tried to cover his adultery and ended up with his hands deep in the murder of Uriah. Though he thought he had covered his tracks, God was watching and sent a prophet to rebuke him. After hearing the message of the prophet and despite his position as king, he responded by quickly humbling himself in repentance.

This character trait of King David stood him out among others. When God gets angry, He never stays that way for long (Micah 7:18). A truly repentant heart always receives His pardon. That means a person who once had the attention of God can again do so.

David was faithful

That David was loyal to God cannot be questioned. His love was repeatedly expressed in the psalms and songs that he wrote. They showed his faithfulness and willingness to serve God, even while he experienced hard conditions.

His writings called on its readers to wait on the Lord, which only faithful people can do (Psalm 27:14). Saul, who was King before David, sought to do his own will and by so doing, disobeyed God. Faithfulness to God involves steadfastness in character and also in service. The one who called us is faithful; His faithfulness is why:

1. His promises are always kept

2. seed and harvest time never cease

3. Our needs are constantly met

4. We enjoy compassion and mercy and

5. We have not been consumed by the devil, among many others.

The faithfulness of God places upon us the responsibility of reciprocity. God expects us to be faithful in our walk with Him too. God saw David's faithfulness even as a boy. He obeyed his father, faithfully cared for the sheep- protecting them from wild beasts, and faithfully played the Harp. All of these brought him before King Saul to serve.

It does not matter whether we are 16 or 40 years old, God demands that we be faithful in whatever we do. Jesus says in the book of Luke that if we can be trusted as faithful in handling little things, then we can also be trusted as faithful in handling big ones. What this means is that in whatever we do (domestic chores, business, schooling or ministry), we must show a high level of commitment and loyalty and strive to hear our Lord say to us at last: "Thou good and faithful servant" (Mathew 25:21).

David sought God's opinion on critical decisions

Every generation should seek the mind of God before taking important and life-impacting decisions because He is an all-knowing God who sees the end from the beginning and has the hearts of kings in his hands. He, by enthroning David, showed that nothing is impossible to Him.

In Bible times, the mind of God was mostly sought concerning issues relating to war. Now, wise people know how delicate and life-impacting decisions that have to do with choosing a career, where to live, how to start a ministry or who to marry can be, so they seek to find out the mind of God before making any move.

David never took such decisions on his own. He always sought the Lord's counsel and direction to deal with challenges. He made enquiries concerning what to do from the Spirit of God through fervent prayer.

Bible records suggest that David was a man of prayer. He inquired of the Lord at least 9 times, as recorded in the first and second Bible books of Samuel. When we seek the will of God on a matter, we show that His opinion counts and it brings Him honour. We also receive His blessing and commitment to ensure the success of the issues we take to Him.

The idea here is that if we develop the kind of attitude that King David had, we will begin to attract God's attention, and it is only then that we will experience His love and loyalty in our lives.

God is always interested in the hearts of men; He is constantly searching for those who are faithful and obedient so that he can through them, show the world his great love and power.

After reading these eleven character traits of David, I am sure that you can see why they made him attract God's attention. If we develop these eleven traits, we can be sure that we will receive the same attention as David and the power that made him become God's favourite.

CHAPTER 9
Dreaming Big

God loves it when his children dream big
-   Christine Caine

Dreams, in this context, refer to all our thoughts, visions and plans for the future. It gives us a sense of achievement and sometimes even gratitude when we can achieve them. I see dreaming big as removing any form of an impediment to the magnitude of whatever we desire. So, whether they are personal dreams- which are specific to just us, or collective ones- which may involve others like our children, family members or the whole community, we must understand that with God, no dream is too big or impossible to make come true.

The starting point of the journey to the land of dream fulfilment is to believe. Yes! Believing that we can be whatever we want and that the one who can make it all possible- God can make it happen. When we fail to realise God's role in making our dreams come true we shortchange ourselves. Also, when we fail to dream very big, we limit God.

Think of who God is and what He has done. Think of His word and the promises it contains. Then hold on to every word that concerns you. It is ill-advised to limit the Holy One of Israel (Psalm 78:14).

A way to know if our dreams are from God is by how people receive them. Our friends and family may all laugh because they, literally speaking, may look at our plans as "Fat jokes". Some may even express to our faces just how impossible and sometimes even ridiculous they think we sound. But deep down, we'll see that we have that buzz- a passion that fills us with excitement and makes us feel very certain.

Trusting the buzz, as being divinely placed inside and working in determination over time, makes things clearer with time, and we begin to see and sense what others do not. What I am talking about here are the possibilities and even the errors. They show us that our dreams are from God.

God wants us to dream big. He wants us to be able to peer into the future with eyes that link to our imaginative hearts. Our eyes, which are gateways to our hearts, can capture images that add content to our hearts and can change our lives forever.

God instructed Moses to look as far as his eyes could see because he and his generation were to receive whatever he saw. That must imply that we ought to visualise to actualise because the visualisation process enables us to connect to the spiritual realm, where the building blocks for the materialisation of thoughts, are laid. All of these lead to the dream manifestations we desire (Genesis 13:15).

MAKING DREAMS COME TRUE

As we strive to make our dreams come true, it might be helpful to be mindful of certain key character traits we can develop as we progress. These traits include but are not limited to the five below. Nevertheless, however, there are a handful of others that can add value to the conversation of making our dreams come true.

Be clear about what you want

Being clear about what you want helps in the visualisation process. It involves identifying your desires and goals and trying to see yourself achieving them.

Visualisation is much like viewing many houses in an estate but isolating a particular one that interests you and putting a fence around it. Multiple dreams can sometimes exist, and each should be separately made clear for easy visualisation.

Write down everything you know about your dream

The next important thing to do is to write down your dreams. Draw tables and diagrams if you must, and include timelines. Writing down all the information we have about an idea or goal ensures we commit them to our subconscious.

The Lord instructed one of His prophets to write down his visions to make them readable and actionable (Habakkuk 2:2). When we write our visions down, they become tangible and remain unaltered until the appointed time of their manifestation.

At times when God speaks prophetically about our dreams, including what the future holds, it is imperative to document His words carefully. Regardless of how impossible your dream may seem initially, writing them down helps connect to them.

I am sure that you have heard about believers who hear from God about their future at a time when what they hear seems very unlikely, yet prayed and worked towards everything they heard because each message was properly documented. It might be necessary to add that writing down our dreams helps us keep them in view until they are finally achieved.

Please do not go and bury dreams or lock them up in a strong box. They must, in their plain form, be kept in constant view to enable regular rumination and prayer until the appointed time of their manifestation. If your dream is to own a mansion for example, I suggest you take a photo of what you want or get a detailed schematic drawing and place them along your daily path, maybe by your dresser. That ensures that the vision stays fresh in your subconscious and increases its likelihood of becoming tangible.

Hold on to your dreams

Many people, while in pursuit of their dreams, become discouraged. They lose focus, maybe due to challenges along the way and even stop believing. Certainly, there will be potholes and bumps along the way, but these should only reinforce the need to keep focus.

We do not all want the same things in life or share the same dreams. God created each of us with peculiar purposes, so no one can tell us that our dreams are not worth pursuing or should try to sell theirs to us. We should hold fast to whatever we want to achieve, however lofty and never give them up. We should take a better position to expand our sights.

While in slavery, the Israelites had one common dream. It was to get out of bitter slavery and Egypt. But after their deliverance, they kept on losing focus and putting limitations on the God of their deliverance.

At each fleeting challenge that they faced, they would begin to complain, whine, gripe, grumble and rebel. God hates these five character traits, and we can be sure that a complainer is certainly ungrateful and quite displeasing. Keeping our minds fixed on our dreams and avoiding the instability that double-mindedness produces is also helpful (James 1:8).

Walk-in love

Jesus spoke about love being the greatest commandment. Firstly, we should love the Lord with our hearts, souls and minds. Then, we are also to love our neighbours as ourselves (Matthew 22:40). For our dreams to come true, we need to maintain a great love relationship with the one who has the power to do it– God. This relationship requires a life of obedience which is the proof of our love (John 14:15) and moves the spirit of God in our favour.

Our love for God is the key that freely unlocks what He has kept in store for us as believers. God can take us beyond our dreams to heights that only the Holy Spirit can reveal. He has prepared packages for His children beyond their dreams and imaginations, and the guarantee they will receive these packages is tied to their love walk (1 Corinthians 2:9).

Surrender your dreams to God

God is at the centre of making dreams come true. His purpose is what stands in our lives. Therefore, no matter the size and nature of our plan, dream or vision, we must place them before Him in prayer (Proverbs 19:21).

We must also realise that God has chosen us for whatever dream we have. So, we may really be destined to make that discovery, invent that software, touch that life etc.

We are not just to come into the world but to come and make an impact that serves God's purpose. He holds the prosperity we seek and can deliver the future we hope for, so trying to achieve any of them without Him makes no sense (Jeremiah 29:11-13).

Fulfilling all our dreams goes beyond acknowledging them. We must put in the hard work – making all those videos and seminar presentations or enduring those long hours. It requires a healthy fear of the Lord, which gives us all the wisdom, understanding and knowledge needed to make our dreams a reality.

The fear of the Lord also releases divine direction and all the necessary resources we need per time to run after our dreams. We must never stop praying while following our dreams because prayer causes the release of answers and revelation, which are usually kept aside for only those who fear the Lord. (Ecclesiastes 5:7 GNV).

CHAPTER 10
Asking Right

"There is no promise God cannot keep, no prayer God will not answer, and no problem too hard for Him to solve"
- Adrian Rogers

When I became the Men's Fellowship President of our headquarters church, I realised that I had taken up an important and challenging task. I would have to do one major thing. That is to find a way to keep men, who are the pillars of society, deeply rooted in Christ.

That would no doubt require finding a way to bring them together and drive them towards full maturity in their walk with Christ. For men to remain relevant to society as providers, husbands and fathers, they must not just develop skills, talents and abilities but ensure that they connect to and stay rooted in Christ Jesus to grow, bear fruit and succeed. All of these are achievable if they allow the word of God to dwell in them richly (John 15:1-6 ESV). Such a decision is highly subjective and powered by a well-developed prayer life.

Men must learn to humble themselves, pray and intercede for one another. They must learn to tap into the power released when they come together, which can strengthen them to succeed where they failed individually. That goes beyond gathering at gardens and pubs but in Christian meetings to dedicate themselves to praying and learning the purpose of God for their lives.

Therefore, since the word of God says: "Go ye therefore, and teach all nations, baptising them in the name of the Father, and the Son, and the Holy Ghost: Teaching them to observe all things whatsoever I have commanded you: and, lo, I am with you always, even to the end of the world" (Matthew 28:19 & 20 KJV). I have put together these last pages as quasi-resource material. It is my contribution to men according to the word of God and our collective growth in Christ.

THE POWER OF PRAYER

There is power released when we pray. The Bible tells us to be sober and watch while we pray (1 Peter 4:7). Whether it is a prayer of intimacy, request, thanksgiving or adoration, it carries enormous power. This power in praying enables us to build relationships and eventually become intimacy with God. It is also a key to His storehouse of blessings.

The power released when a righteous man prays cannot be measured. The ear of God always listens to a man who is obedient to His word. When the heart of such a man fills with expectation, there is always a powerful release from the supernatural to grant them (Proverbs 10:24). Therefore, the power in praying is more potent in the life of people who avoid sin and who daily live to please God.

Faith is an invaluable part of a strong prayer life. The stronger it is, the easier our ability to stay calm and patient, knowing that the Father has heard us and is working something out for us (Psalm 40:1).

When I needed a job at one time, I prayed and was sure that the Lord heard me because I heard Him say that He would give me the job I asked for. However, after six months, nothing! My faith began to shake until my pastor told me in counsel to go and wait patiently.

In 2020, our church taught intensively and extensively on thanksgiving. I know that thankfulness carries a certain power, triggered during the show of appreciation and which draws more from the giver. It is okay to desire things but not to worry stressfully about them. We should ask for what we need after thanking God for His previous goodness.

Living in thanksgiving cannot be separated from our prayer lives if we must move the Father to action. It does not just show our appreciation and draws more from God but also shows our realisation that God is sovereign and the giver of all things (Philippians 4:6).

THE BENEFITS OF PRAYER

You will agree that one way to build a relationship is through communication. Prayer is our way of communicating with God. It draws us closer to Him and should start with thanksgiving, followed by a dialogue - during which we speak to God and listen to Him respond to us. This kind of communication builds our spiritual sensitivity and draws from above the revelation we require (Jeremiah 33:3).

Men should always pray (1 Chronicles 16:11). It is the only way to line-up our judgements and plans with the mind of God. Whether individually or as a group, the Bible advises all men to seek an understanding of the will of God (Ephesians 5:17) because it is the best for us (Jeremiah 29:11).

Also, as we build our prayer lives, it is interesting to acknowledge that God responds to us considering His will concerning our lives (1 John 5:14-15). Jesus, who ought to be our example while on earth, was always interested in doing only the will of The Father, which can be revealed by hearing the word of God and praying fervently.

Prayer releases God's blessings.

God wants to prosper His children and have us live lives free from harm and prosperity filled. He also wants us to live lives full of the hope that our future will be rich in His favour. He spoke this through His prophet- Jeremiah, and I have come to realise, over time, that the plan of God, as stipulated in the book of Jeremiah, has not changed (Jeremiah 29:11). It is our responsibility to connect to it. Prayer is a defence and a shield for every child of God.

Satan and his agents are bound and kept away through fervent and constant praying. The Bible assures obedient men that whenever they make decrees, they shall stand because God is sure to honour them.

All we need to do when we pray is to take whatever the word of God says on a matter and stand on it. That will give us victory even amid the cruellest work of darkness that may be in operation around us. In times of trouble and distress, praying brings deliverance.

When the storm raged, Jesus assuaged the raging winds and angry waters. He commanded them to be still, and they obeyed. Also, when God's people cried out to God in their trouble, as recorded in the Psalms, He delivered them from their distress and made the storm keep still and the waves of the sea hush. That made the people of God glad (Psalm 107:28-30).

Prayer brings healing.

In the name of Jesus, power was released by the Holy Spirit to the disciples to heal the sick. That same power is still available to us today. The Bible instructs sick people among us to call the church elders to pray over them and anoint them with oil in the name of the Lord. (James 5:14). That is why we witness many people receive healing during Healing or Annointing Services in our churches.

Great miracles occur through praying.

Bible records do not contain accounts of healing from sicknesses and infirmities through the power of prayer alone but also of mighty works of miracles. Mighty miracles refer to stories like when Jesus fed the multitude with fish and loaves of bread and when Peter asked to be allowed to kneel and pray for Tabitha – what followed this was a miracle (Acts 9:40).

THE CONCEPT OF CORPORATE PRAYER

Now let us consider Corporate Praying. This kind of prayer involves praying with others (one or more people). It is a powerful way to pray. It allows us to join our faith with others to receive what we ask from God.

Jesus says that if two people on earth agree about anything they ask for, it will be done for them by His Father in heaven and goes further to explain that where two or three gather in His name, He is there with them (Matthew 18:19-20).

The keyword here, through which Corporate Prayer thrives, is: "Agreement". A simple way to explain the agreement is to look at it as a time when people gather with one focus and the common expectation of one outcome.

When more than one person gathers for the sake of Christ Jesus, He says He comes into their midst. Now, does this not give us hope of getting the answers we need - when the giver is right there with us? That is why there is tremendous power released during a prayer of agreement.

We can benefit from the power released when two or more people come together to pray. As Christians, when we gather and join our faith together to pray, it is a time when the release of power from the Holy Spirit occurs (Hebrews 10:25).

Many churches today, during services, take time to pray in one accord concerning particular needs identified and still run special prayer groups that meet on stipulated days to pray.

My church still has what is called a Prayer Band. It is the gathering of Prayer Warriors in meetings where you can experience the manifestation of the power of the Holy Spirit. Men ought to gather and pray and must be encouraged to do so.

The coming together of brethren as prayer partners have encouraged fellowship, developed faith and promoted selflessness. This practice may not be as common as it used to be, but it is still an acceptable Christian practice across churches. These days, praying has been taken from its widely known arenas and participants to something new and spreading. It is the practice of online praying. They are special prayer sessions focused on specific needs, which are getting very popular nowadays. Online evangelists take advantage of many online apps for this purpose.

THREE BENEFITS OF CORPORATE PRAYER

For many years of my life I had skipped church gatherings and missed the benefits of praying together with other Christians. It was not until I discovered the power of corporate fellowship that I understood the magnitude of what I had missed all those years.

I have taken the time to document the benefits of praying together with other Christians to encourage people like me, who did not take advantage of Christian gatherings, and enjoy its benefits.

It releases the glory of the Lord instantly

Since Jesus says that where two or three gather in His name, He will also there (Mathew 18:20). It is therefore quite acceptable to gather at prayer places, with the assurance that Jesus comes on the scene and oh! What great hope we have that He hears and answers instantly

It increases faith

Sometimes faith may be missing or not up to the size of the mustard seed spoken about by Jesus in the Bible. The rebuke He gave His disciples when He said: "Oh ye of little faith" (Mathew 8:26), remains relevant even today.

One way to increase faith is simply to add more. Jesus still says to us today that faith as small as a mustard seed can make anything possible (Mathew

17:20). Coming together to pray with others helps increase faith needed to draw the answers we desire.

Therefore, just imagine a situation where three people gather to pray for something, and between them, one person stands without any faith while the remaining two stand with mustard seed-sized faith. Now, won't the doubt of the one without faith be affected by the mustard seed faith of the others? Would this not lead to an increase in the quantity of faith they generate as a group? They would certainly get the answers that they need, won't they? (James 1:6-8)

It strengthens and builds

The Bible says that we should share our burdens (Galatians 6:2). By doing that, we help bring relief and strength to everyone because it is easier to bear them as a group.

Praying together can help build others up. In line with the Bible passage that says that iron sharpens iron, we are confident that one person sharpens another in faith (Proverbs 27:17). We can also learn how to pray and receive from God if we pray together.

THE LIMIT TO WHICH GOD ANSWERS PRAYERS

God has limitless wisdom and power that make Him able to exceed our expectations when answering our prayers. The Bible says:

Now unto him that is able to do exceeding abundantly above all that we ask or think, according to the power that worketh in us,"(Ephesians 3:20 KJV). Two pertinent parts of this scripture are: "Above all, we can ask for or think" And: "the power that worketh in us". So let us decipher what these two parts of the scripture means to ascertain the limit to which God answers prayers.

Above all, we can ask or think

Before we request from God, He already knows what we need and has made provision. That is why walking in His will is so important, since whenever we do His will, He provides for us.

Now let me point out what the exceedingly and abundantly in the quote above means. It comes from considering the life of Solomon, who asked God for wisdom to rule the Lord's people and got more than he requested. He got wealth and peace in addition.

One day the Lord was so pleased with me that He asked me what I wanted Him to do for me. I thought hard and made a "smart" request, but He said: "I will give you a car". That promise made me wonder because I already had a car. You see, what I could not see was the near future in which I would lose my car, so in addition to my "smart" request, God took care of some of my future too. He gave me more than I asked for.

According to the power that worketh in us

When the power of God enters a man's life, it causes the miraculous to occur. This power, which is the same one that raised Jesus from death, is released through the Spirit of God, also known as the Holy Spirit (Luke 1:35).

That awesome power that raised Jesus, is what He was talking about when He responded to a question asked by those who asked him a question. He said these words to them: "Your mistake is that you don't know the scriptures and you don't know the power of God" (Mathew 22:29).

Jesus knew the importance of this power while He carried out His earthly ministry and told His disciples to wait for the Holy Spirit, who would empower them and for whom they should return to Jerusalem.

We must allow the Holy Spirit to fill us with the power of God which once activated in our lives, makes us able to attract and do the miraculous, like it did in the life of Christ Jesus.

THE SECRET TO ANSWERED PRAYER

I learned the secret to getting prayers answered every time, and since the day I discovered this powerful secret, I have taught it and lived it. You see, Jesus explains to us through His word that the reason why many of us do not have, is because we do not ask.

Also, when we pray, we must be persistent in our belief that God has heard us because He always does and answers.

Jesus also taught us that if we ask, we shall receive what we ask for. He even went further to talk about how faithful and able our Father in heaven is, to give good things to those who ask Him and that God does not give His children destructive gifts. They certainly won't ask Him for bread, and He gives them a stone (Matthew 7:7-12).

Many people have asked how they would know if their prayers have been answered when they kneel to pray. It is a faith thing, and we know that we have received or that we are on the right path by His Spirit who gives us peace. He fills our hearts in and out with joy and peace on whatever matter, so that we may overflow with hope by His mighty power (Romans 15:13).

Pray according to God's will always

Praying according to the will of God guarantees that we receive the answers to our prayers because by doing so, we submit to Him and prove ourselves to be obedient children, which pleases Him and causes Him to hear us (1 John 5:14-15).

I recall always being challenged by having to find what the will of God was for my life, which I eventually discovered to be quite different from what

I had initially planned for myself. I eventually discovered what it was through His word.

The will of God concerning a person is known through the word of God. That usually follows an earnest desire to find it out or a search. Just as it was in the life of Abraham (Genesis 15), the visiting angels released the word of God, which powerfully contained His will.

Be in communion with the Lord always

Communion with Christ Jesus, I discovered, involves having a special relationship with Him. It should be a love relationship that involves: obedience, faithfulness, trust, reverence, service and constant communication, just as it would in any healthy relationship between two people.

Jesus makes us understand that the secret to getting all our prayers answered is hinged together with two important principles, which are:

1. The quality of our relationship with Him and

2. Asking in line with the will of God through an in-filling of the word of God in us (John 15:7 KJV).

Forgive offences before praying

Forgiveness takes away the intention to punish others for the wrong that they do, especially to us. Morally speaking, it is an act we should demand if we have forgiven others.

The Lord taught His disciples about the empathy practised when we do this during a prayer lesson (Luke 11:2-4). He taught them to say: "Forgive us our trespasses as we forgive those who trespass against us" Which further strengthens the morality in forgiveness, making it clear that we are undeserving of forgiveness if we do not forgive others (Mathew 7:12)

Embrace the power of righteousness

There is great power in righteousness. "Righteousness is like a shield of protection, guarding those who keep their integrity, but sin is the downfall of the wicked" (Proverbs 13:6). This downfall is certain because the Lord does not connect to sinners and is usually far from them. Even their prayers are ignored by God (Proverbs 15:8) because they are considered abominable (Proverbs 28:9 KJV).

God is always interested in the lives of those who live righteously and commits to answering them when they pray (1 Peter 3:12). There is great power released when a righteous man prays continuously with his whole heart about a matter (James 5:16).

Believe in your heart for an answer

Now, God is a spirit. He is omnipresent. No one can claim to have seen Him, but we know by faith that He exists. When the righteous pray, God says He inclines

His ears to their prayers. He has even made us know that He hears what we ask in our hearts (Jeremiah 17:10).

Therefore, that He hears our prayers is not contestable but do we feel heard when we pray? You see, that we even believe that God exists and He can help us is, "Big faith" And nothing shall be impossible for people who believe. Jesus tells us that when we pray, we should believe we have received whatever we ask for. If we do that, whatever we ask will be ours Mark 11:24).

To believe, we must act as if we have already received it by thanksgiving and do all the things that we would have done if we asked for a plane ticket and it suddenly dropped right before us. Yes, that's right, start packing!

Realise that we do not know how to pray

That might sound a bit contradictory or confusing but if you have ever felt sad or weak, then you might understand better. God does not want us to do anything on our own. He wants us to pray according to His will and rely on His spirit for everything.

He loves and cares so much for us that even if we do not know what to say when we pray, probably because we are so weak, sad or distraught, the Holy Spirit intercedes for us.

God, as written earlier, hears our hearts. He also knows us better than we know ourselves. So, depending on Him when we pray is the way to go and drives away doubt and fear. It brings us closer to a God that loves us so much (Romans 8:26).

Now, let us look at John 15:7. Jesus, in that scripture, tried to open up our understanding by revealing the secret to getting our prayers answered. He talked about abiding in Him and His word abiding in us if we want answers to every prayer. Understanding what all that means is such a big deal and can help us get the answers we seek to all our prayers.

To abide in Christ is to have a relationship with Him, while to have His word abide in us, is to be filled with the word of God (spoken or written). Subsequently, due to how powerful these principles

The Secret to Answered Prayer

are, let us dig deeper into them so we can put them into better practice in our everyday Christian walk.

What does it mean to abide in Christ?

To abide in Christ means to remain in Him. It also refers to living a life of constant communion with Him. That is a life of obedience and constantly seeking to do the will of the Father. It is a life lived in total submission, having been crucified with Christ such that we no longer live our lives based on our terms but on His (Galatians 2:20).

Such a life is one in which we show an awareness and influence of the finished work of redemption on the cross. We acknowledge the son of God and rejoice continuously over His love for us which led to His death. It also requires praying continually and giving thanks in all situations (1 Thessalonians 5:16-18).

What does it mean for His words to abide in us?

The Bible says in the book of Hebrews that the word of God is alive and active. It has power to lead us to the will of God concerning our lives or any other matter. David testified to opening up his heart to the word, and we ought to do so too.

The New Testament instructs us to let the word of Christ dwell in us richly (Colossians 3:16). That means that we must, like the early translations of the Bible says, "Hearken"- A word that means to hear, meditate on and obey.

Jesus, also known as the "Word" Stands at the door of the heart of men and knocks, and if anyone hears His voice and opens the door, He will come in, and they will eat together (Revelation 3:20).

Whether or not to open the door of our hearts to Jesus is the most transformative decision we can ever make. It is guaranteed to change our lives forever.

-End-

Additional Information

For questions, requests and comments, please send an email to: ubong.tommy@hotmail.com

Also, to order this book, please email the address above. You can also visit any of the following stores:

http://amazon.com/author/u.k.tommy

https://selar.co/rir6

https://store.okadabooks.comm/book/about/1_am_g lory/43698